Delivering Satisfaction
AND
Service Quality

A CUSTOMER-BASED
APPROACH FOR LIBRARIES

Peter Hernon
and
John R. Whitman

AMERICAN LIBRARY ASSOCIATION

Chicago and London

2001

Project editor: Joan A. Grygel

Cover: Tessing Design

Text design: Dianne M. Rooney

Composition by the dotted i in Janson Text and Univers using QuarkXPress 4.04
for Macintosh

Printed on 50-pound white offset, a pH-neutral stock, and bound in
10-point coated cover stock by McNaughton & Gunn

The paper used in this publication meets the minimum requirements of American National
Standard for Information Sciences—Permanence of Paper for Printed Library Materials,
ANSI Z39.48-1992. ⊚

Library of Congress Cataloging-in-Publication Data

Hernon, Peter.
    Delivering satisfaction and service quality : a customer-based approach for libraries /
Peter Hernon, John R. Whitman.
      p.   cm.
    Includes bibliographical references (p.) and index.
    ISBN 0-8389-0789-X (alk. paper)
    1. Reference services (Libraries)—United States—Management. 2. Consumer
satisfaction—United States. I. Whitman, John R. II. Title.
Z711.H455 2000
025.5′2—dc21
                                      00-044811

Printed in the United States of America.

05 04 03 02 01   5 4 3 2 1

Contents

Figures

Tables

Preface

Business enterprises—those having survived a decade of sometimes painful reengineering to stay competitive in a global economy—now view satisfying the customer as a core business value. They came to this realization by recognizing that customers have choices and by understanding that customers are won and kept through developing relationships of sustained value to the customer.

Customer-related performance is now deemed so critical that the Malcolm Baldrige National Quality Award (created by Public Law 100-107, 1987) values customer and market knowledge, customer satisfaction, and customer-focused results, as a combination, higher than any other single measure for the award.[1]

Attention to the customer has not been lost among other institutions, including noncommercial ones, in particular, libraries. But libraries are not exactly in competition with each other for survival in a global marketplace. So what is driving this intense and pervasive, if not perverse, focus on the customer? The answer may be that libraries, too, are beginning to recognize that customers have choices for their information needs and that some of these choices are drawing customers away from the library in increasing numbers, and perhaps for good. The Internet, and its almost unlimited potential, mindless convenience, and ultracheap (if not free) access, looms large as a competitive information resource.

So what are librarians to do? For answers, we can turn to the experience of business and see how it may apply to libraries. Central to this issue is the relationship between the library and its users, or, in increasingly common—and appropriate—parlance, its customers. The first step toward getting a grip is to recognize and examine this relationship for what it is: a transaction between the library, as a service-delivery enterprise, and the consumer of its services, its customer. Once this relationship, which we call the "satisfaction relationship," is established and understood, the ensuing challenge is to take control of managing this relationship in a way that is healthy and ensures the continued, mutual satisfaction of both customer and library. The prospect of managing the satisfaction relationship is not only attainable by today's library leaders but the possibilities it affords for creating the future of libraries are immensely exciting.

The subject of service delivery as it pertains to libraries can be broken into two related components: service quality and customer satisfaction. *Assessing Service Quality*, published by the American Library Association in 1998,[2] may be considered the companion volume for the present book. The primary audience of the present volume, like that of the preceding book, includes not only librarians in leadership roles, specifically middle and upper management, but also all librarians, members of library boards, funders of libraries, governmental and nongovernmental policy makers concerned with libraries, and students in library and information science programs.

Delivering Satisfaction and Service Quality provides a conceptual framework that should prove useful in understanding, thinking, and talking about service quality and customer satisfaction, what they are, how they are shaped, and how they can evolve subject to both internal, controllable forces and external, uncontrollable factors. This model promises a foundation on which a library can actually define and set customer expectations in a way necessary to deliver high quality service and satisfaction. The book describes a plan for providing satisfying service that virtually any type of library—academic, public, corporate, or special—can adopt and adapt to its circumstances.

Unlike generic business books on customer satisfaction, no matter how persuasive their arguments in favor of satisfying the customer, the present volume provides specific, practical instruments that may be employed to measure service quality and customer satisfaction. These instruments have been tried and tested with repeated success, and, in the case of the satisfaction questionnaires, may be used as is, with little customization required. This book, then, provides a way of thinking about managing service quality and customer satisfaction, and, together with *Assessing Service Quality*, it places the tools to do so directly in the hands of librarians who can put them to use immediately, without further academic or skills training.

Delivering Satisfaction and Service Quality also provides an overview of how technology, particularly personal computer software and the Internet, may be used in the customer satisfaction survey process. It lists specific software that can be used in conjunction with the offered survey instruments, making implementing the service plan even more accessible. A section on analyzing survey results provides specific examples of the types of analyses that might be performed on assessment data, requiring no specialized training in statistics, and further equips the librarian with the means to become immediately productive.

Taken together, this book and *Assessing Service Quality* provide the library with a solid foundation on which to address service quality and customer satisfaction as they pertain to a library. While the focus is on becoming immediately productive, the model offered should remain viable well into the future. In fact, a tenet of this book is that, by using the conceptual and practical tools offered here, the library will be in a far stronger position to shape its future based on managing its relationship with the customer through times of rapid and unprecedented change.

As collaborating authors, we have enjoyed the process of combining an academic and business approach to understanding the model underlying service quality and customer satisfaction in libraries. One of us brings to bear years of experience in teaching, research, and consulting, primarily to academic libraries in the United States and New Zealand. The other offers specific and practical tools, including most of the survey instruments and software packages described in these pages, which have been used both in commercial enterprises and predominantly in public libraries. It should be noted that several of these survey instruments are owned by his employer, and his company also has a financial interest in some of the software products described herein. However, rather than detract from the merit of this contribution, this connection is intended to add credibility to what works in the real world and can be usefully applied again and again with satisfaction guaranteed.

Of course, the success in applying the principles, procedures, and tools offered in this book will ultimately be measured not only in terms of the library's demonstrated ability to achieve the desired satisfaction scores among its present and prospective customers but also in the ability to evolve a mission that ensures a steadfastly prized place for the library in a rapidly changing environment far into the future. These outcomes are of substantial interest to the authors, and any feedback on results as well as comments and suggestions on the process would be welcome indeed.

NOTES

1. "Baldrige National Quality Program, Criteria for Performance Excellence 2000," see http://www.nist.gov (accessed April 18, 2000).
2. Peter Hernon and Ellen Altman, *Assessing Service Quality: Satisfying the Expectations of Library Customers* (Chicago: American Library Assn., 1998).

Acknowledgments

We wish to thank Ellen Altman and Danuta A. Nitecki for their critical reading of a draft of the manuscript. We also appreciate the many helpful suggestions of Timothy Jones. In addition, we gratefully acknowledge the following sources:

Chapter 1

Bernd Stauss and Christian Friege, "Regaining Service Customers," Journal of Service Research (vol. 1, no. 4). Page 349, copyright © 1999 by Sage Publications, Inc. Reprinted by Permission of Sage Publications, Inc.

Figure 1.4, "Common Customer Service Complaints." Adapted with the permission of The Free Press, a Division of Simon & Schuster, from DISCOVERING THE SOUL OF SERVICE: The Nine Drivers of Sustainable Business Success by Leonard L. Berry. Copyright © 1999 by Leonard L. Berry.

Chapter 2

1994, The Haworth Press, Inc., Binghamton, New York. Journal of Customer Services in Marketing & Management. Marla Joyce Stafford, "A Normative Model for Improving Services Quality," 1, no. 1, pp. 17, 18, 19.

Chapter 4

Prioritizing Academic Programs and Services: Reallocating Resources to Achieve Strategic Balance. Robert C. Dickeson. Copyright © 1999, Jossey-Bass, Inc. Reprinted by permission of Jossey-Bass, Inc., a subsidiary of John Wiley & Sons, Inc.

"Appendix: Examples from the Literature," Karen V. Bottrill and Victor M. H. Borden. *New Directions for Institutional Research.* Copyright © 1994, Jossey-Bass, Inc. Reprinted by permission of Jossey-Bass, Inc., a subsidiary of John Wiley & Sons, Inc.

Chapter 6

The Public Library Satisfaction Questionnaire, the Academic Library Questionnaire, the Staff Satisfaction Questionnaire, and the Workshop Evaluation
Questionnaire are used with permission of Surveytools Corporation. The
company allows use of these questionnaires on an as-is basis, or with modifications, provided that the questionnaires are used by libraries that purchase
this book, that the questionnaires will not be used to generate any income,
and that the Surveytools copyright is protected. If any of these questionnaires
are used, the following notice must be included on the questionnaire: Form
Copyright © by Surveytools Corporation. ALL RIGHTS RESERVED.

Chapter 9

Pages 22–23, 26, the ten dimensions of service quality. Adapted with the permission
of The Free Press, a Division of Simon & Schuster, from DELIVERING
QUALITY SERVICE: Balancing Customer Perceptions by Valarie A. Zeithaml, A. Parasuraman, Leonard L. Berry. Copyright © 1990 by The Free Press.

1

Understanding Customer Service

People come first.[1]

Librarians should be creating their future and not having someone else do it.[2]

Customer service has been characterized "as meeting the needs and expectations of the customers as defined by the customers."[3] Meeting those needs and expectations means that librarians know about and are attuned to those needs and expectations and are willing to meet high-interest expectations consistently and well. Most importantly, the customer, as the consumer of library services, does not define the library's mission and its service delivery. The library sets this framework but is sensitive to its customers' expectations. The organization's vision of its service role (and its inability to do everything for everyone well despite its best intentions) must ultimately guide what services are offered and how they are offered. Nonetheless, because customers should help to shape the services that libraries provide and the view of what libraries do successfully, it is important for librarians to listen to customers. Susan Smith stresses that "to know what your customers want, you've got to ask them!" As she explains,

> *Defined by the customer* is a very important point to get because it says that if the customer doesn't perceive you as offering good customer service, then [at least

to that customer] you aren't. The customer is the judge here. No matter how good your internal records claim you are, the customer is the only voice worth listening to. So in order to have an effective customer service initiative, you must know what your customers want, provide it to them consistently, and ask them how you're doing.[4]

Thus, metrics such as the number of customers served; reference questions asked and answered; and items checked out, borrowed, and lent are useful but are still no substitute for listening to customers tell about their expectations and satisfactions as the library implements and refines its service vision.

It is not the intention of this chapter to defend the use of the word "customer" and its relevance to libraries. Such a rationale has been provided elsewhere.[5] Suffice it to say, the word *customer* dispels the myth of the free library and substitutes a more accurate metaphor for service at a time when "the library is in increasingly tight competition for declining resources, and unless it adopts and masters the language and techniques of its competitors, it faces a future of declining support and significance."[6]

Irene B. Hoadley, when discussing today's libraries, observes that they "are run in a more business-like way." She raises the question "What is operating in a business-like way?" and then answers:

> It means there is a more formalized structure, concern with *accountability* [authors' emphasis] and money management and an emphasis on efficiency. . . . To say a library is run like a business almost always carries a negative connotation. . . . This should not be the case because there are business principles that can benefit how libraries are run. . . . Better accounting and money management are benefits to libraries. Another is the accountability characteristic of business operations that requires self-examination to determine if what is being done is what really benefits the organization and those it serves.[7]

Service to Customers

Librarians manage information resources (the selection, collection, organization, dissemination, and preservation of resources usually created by external agents and agencies such as authors, publishers, corporate institutions, and governments) for a purpose—their use by customers. Customers are not a monolithic, homogeneous group; rather, there are customer segments such as college and university students and faculty; elementary, secondary, and trade school students; the elderly; businesspeople; and so forth. (These segments might appear within multiethnic communities.)

A number of customers may not request or require assistance, preferring instead to find resources on their own or to rely on friends or colleagues for information gathering and evaluation. Nonetheless, it is important to remember that "every contact a customer makes within the library is an opportunity for the customer to form an opinion. . . . When . . . [these] 'moments of truth' go unmanaged, the quality of service regresses to mediocrity."[8] Managing these moments effectively involves a long-term and well-thought-out commitment from the organization and individual staff members.

As shown in figure 1.1, libraries, like other service organizations, serve present customers. They might also try to attract prospective or never-gained customers (e.g., incoming freshmen or families that have recently moved into the community) and even some lost customers. Since there will always be non- and lost customers who will resist any overtures from libraries, library management must decide whether to try to regain lost customers. Any decision will require "a systematic and differentiated analysis of the customer value," or a calculation of regaining costs and benefits.[9] It is most important to serve existing customers and to reach out to never-gained customers. Lost customers should not be ignored, but the library may have to deal with them on an individual basis, once the staff realize that these individuals indeed may have left the area or have found alternative sources of information that they prefer to use.

FIGURE 1.1
Customer Management

Prospective or Never-Gained Customers	Present Customers	Lost Customers
No present relationship with library	Has a relationship with library	Relationship ended
No previous experience with the particular library	Has experience with the library	Had experience with the library
→	↑ ↓	←
Traditional Recruitment	**Retention Management**	**Regain Management**
More or less targeted marketing in which the main communication is aimed at attracting and inviting use	Often focused on regular customers, ones who might become "loyal"	Often highly selective and focused on certain customers, ones receptive to two-way communication

Adapted from Bernd Stauss and Christian Friege, "Regaining Service Customers," *Journal of Service Research* 1, no. 4 (May 1999): 349. Copyright © 1999 by Sage Publications, Inc. Reprinted by permission of Sage Publications, Inc.

Technology as an Enhancement of Customer Service

Technology offers a means to improve internal communication, productivity, and efficiency within the organization; to provide seamless service to customers; to create new and more effective service delivery; and to enhance customer satisfaction. At the same time, there are segments of the population that do not feel comfortable with technology and that regard it as a service barrier. A challenge is to introduce and maintain relevant services, to work to overcome such barriers, and to ensure that these individuals obtain the needed resources.

Technology as a change agent represents opportunities as well as challenges, as more libraries divert resources to the provision of electronic services and as they seek to serve customers who do not physically visit library buildings. "How much should be reallocated and at what pace?"[10] Customers might send reference questions by e-mail, engage in document request and delivery via the online public access catalog (OPAC), search periodical indexes and databases remotely and gain full-text access to titles immediately, and so forth. Libraries create partnerships with, for instance, other libraries, campuses, and communities in order to improve the breadth of information access and the speed of document delivery. As a result, information access increases and library ownership of resources declines, and in-house statistics (e.g., number of reference questions asked) may also decline, whereas statistics reflecting remote access may dramatically increase. An unintended but real consequence of access to more information is *information overload*—having access to more information than the individual can or is willing to cope with. Herein is a challenge for the profession to resolve.

Another challenge is that "although many campuses have defined initial approaches to offering courses over the Internet, few, if any, have defined a scalable and viable strategy for making library resources available to these "distant" learners."[11] In addition, digital libraries, which offer "more kinds of information resources than . . . [does] the traditional library" (e.g., "scholarly materials, popular Web sites, museum objects, multimedia presentations, quantitative data, and working papers"), as well as the impact technology has on library staff, operations, and services, do not represent the only changes facing libraries.[12] Susan Rosenblatt mentions that customer expectations are also changing. Researchers, for instance, "expect books and print journals to be available as quickly as are online catalog records and online journals." Furthermore, she states,

> As IT [information technology] puts increasing percentages of relevant information resources on the scholar's desk rather than on library shelves, reliance on print collections and services is increasingly less compelling, even for faculty. Thus, demand for high-quality print materials housed in the library may decline once online information is adequate for most research needs. . . .
>
> The experience of the digital library user will influence expectations for other library services. Many will prefer self-service over mediated services. For example, instead of standing in line at a circulation desk, borrowers expect to

use a circulation kiosk and renew library books online; they prefer to submit document-delivery requests online directly to suppliers rather than visit the interlibrary lending service. Similarly, when a critical mass of reference tools is available online, digital library users will expect to ask questions over the Internet rather than go to the reference desk, even during hours that the library is open.[13]

As a consequence, customers can gain access to electronic resources twenty-four hours a day, seven days a week, even when the library building is closed.

Core Values, Customers, and Staff

Leonard L. Berry, who analyzed "great service companies," concluded that they held certain "core values: excellence, innovation, joy, teamwork, respect, integrity, and social profit."[14] If one could define "social profit" in the context of an enriched life gained from the use of information and knowledge or the conversion of information into knowledge, that term might have relevance to libraries. At any rate, these core values serve as a reminder that a library, like any great service company, must build outward, producing a motivated staff committed to (and empowered to give) service excellence. Berry regards excellence as "a defining value."[15] As such, service quality and satisfaction look at that value from the perspective of customers and what they regard as important. Libraries embracing such concepts, however, must embrace change.

Change

As Darlene E. Weingand correctly notes,

> Too often, organizational culture is rooted in tradition and habit, and change is often an unwelcome visitor. Yet, change is today's one constant, and no organization can escape its presence and effects. Whether regarded as an opportunity or as a threat, the specter of change sits on every organization's board of directors; the library is no exception. . . .
>
> Libraries that cling to traditional models of operation or elect to maintain the status quo will proceed slowly and laboriously . . . , relating less and less to their customers, and ultimately losing the support needed to continue operations. These are the libraries that hold fast to a view of library service that still connects to yesterday's paradigms. The library's management has lost sight of the many changes in customer needs and expectations. To survive, an organization must adapt; if it does not adapt, it cannot ensure—or assume—survival.[16]

By modifying the approach to service offered by Weingand, we present the approach emphasized by this book:

How can the library create and maintain *excellence* in a *changing environment* when considering *service quality* and *customer satisfaction* as essential for *survival* and *prosperity?*[17]

The key words and phrases that appear in italicized type in this question are essential elements of customer service: *Excellence (E)*, *Changing Environment (CE)*, *Service Quality (SQ)*, *Customer Satisfaction (CS)*, *Survival (S)*, and *Prosperity (P)*. Implicit to achieving *SQ* and *CS* is the *Library's Vision (LV)*. Although these different words and phrases can be presented as an equation, in practice, such an equation lacks mathematical precision; after all, customer service involves subjectivity:

$$\text{Customer Service in } CE \text{ leading to } S \text{ and } P = E(SQ + CS) - LV$$

E and LV must balance for the library to achieve customer service. If E exceeds LV, customer service rises in value accordingly; however, if LV is greater than E, customer service diminishes.

"Unless planning takes place with the customer as the pivot point," as Weingand notes, planning "cannot carry the library forward vigorously into the next century." Figure 1.2 "shows the differences in customer service in libraries that heed the traditional paradigm and libraries that focus on the customer."[18] Clearly, libraries must reach some balance among the expectations and opinions of their customers (those who actually use or are likely to use library services) and staff as well as stakeholders as they strive to achieve their stated mission and vision. (Stakeholders are those who have an interest in the organization, usually financial; they may exert influence, primarily through funding or legislative oversight, but they are not customers.) In doing this, both staff and customers must be kept informed about that balance and the progress toward reaching stated goals so that they remain involved and committed to providing an ongoing flow of information to the organization. The goal is to have both customers and staff expect to know how things are going and where the organization is headed.

In defining customer service, the onus is on the library's senior management team to deliver service based on demonstrated customer expectations. Management also must be innovative in ways that can set new expectations among existing customers and expand the customer base—including more customer segments—over time.

This vision is executed through the library's mission and requires customer feedback, whereby the customer ultimately indicates whether he or she is satisfied. The feedback from the customer provides the library with the necessary insight into how well the vision is being achieved, in terms of both traditional and innovative service delivery. Obviously, any data collected must be meaningful to (and used by) the organization.

An important ingredient in achieving the type of inspiration that will enrich a library's vision is an understanding of how the process of change affects the library and the customer. Change also affects the staff; their empowerment means that the demands placed on them will be greater. As a consequence, the library will "require a better informed and knowledgeable staff. As the staff . . . [become] a functioning, rather than a static, part of the organization, the culture of the organization changes, as does the role of the staff."[19]

FIGURE 1.2
The Change Equation

Factor	Worst Case	Best Case
1. Excellence	Customers often hear: "We don't have it" . . . period.	Customers always hear: "That item is not available today, but we can get it for you."
2. Changing Environment	School and academic libraries in town have Internet capability, but the public library does not.	The library is actively involved in the local freenet and also offers Internet access on site.
3. Service Quality	Staff assume they already know the customer's expectations—more resources and longer hours of operation.	Using various techniques, staff listen to customers and anticipate expectations (for example, Web services). Staff view complaints as opportunities to improve and delight customers.
4. Customer Satisfaction	Staff are indifferent to customers and their satisfaction—after all, there will always be a need for libraries.	Staff are not satisfied with the status quo, and management invests in staff.
5. Customer Service	The staff favors staff convenience over customer convenience. Staff are often abrupt and appear to be overly busy.	The library offers a dial-in public access catalog that also allows customers to request reserves and interlibrary loans. Materials are delivered to special locations in town where customers can retrieve them during convenient hours. Information is transmitted to customers by e-mail.
6. Survival	Many customers now use the services of the library in the neighboring town.	The library is enthusiastically regarded by the community.
7. Prosperity	The library receives declining support from the community.	A new building is overwhelmingly approved. Citizens regard serving on the library board as an honor.

Factors 1–2 and 5–7 from Darlene E. Weingand, *Customer Service Excellence: A Concise Guide for Librarians* (Chicago: American Library Assn., 1997), 10.

Best Practices

Best practices are the means by which leading organizations achieve top performance, and they serve as goals for other organizations striving for excellence. Best practices encourage change and improvement, and they reward staff for their innovations. Such practices involve recognition (e.g., perhaps awards and mentions in newspapers and the literature) for Web sites and other customer services. Recognition may be granted by the

American Library Association and other professional associations and societies, local or state government, and so forth. Recognition gives staff a sense of accomplishment and pride and makes them more receptive to soliciting customer feedback, especially if it is constructive and assists the organization in improving its service performance.

By focusing on best practices, senior management must assume strong leadership and make staff realize that they are responsible for their results, not just their efforts. In other words, the intent is to create a performance-based organization that is forward thinking and that reviews the best practices of competitive organizations for possible adoption. These practices may, however, have to undergo some change before adoption.

Competition

In an increasingly competitive environment, the private sector has discovered that superior customer service results in market advantage. Thus, companies strive to improve customer service and to develop strong, ongoing relationships with customers. Best-practice companies capitalize on opportunities to build a strong relationship in the first contact with new customers. Although libraries do not comprise a private-sector business, they face competition (e.g., bookstores, the Internet, document-delivery firms, and vendors of electronic resources). Competition is not limited to formal providers of information and knowledge; it also extends to informal providers of oral and visual communication (e.g., friends, colleagues, and gatekeepers, or individuals within certain ethnic communities who serve as links to the information resources required by community residents).[20] Librarians concerned about attracting, retaining, and better serving customers in a competitive environment ought to consider questions such as:

> What do customers value when they choose the services of competing organizations?
>
> How do customers rate the performance of the library in relationship to its competitors?
>
> How do the answers to both of these questions affect customer perceptions of value—or how people choose among competitors? Furthermore, how do the answers to these questions affect customers' choices about whether to continue using the library in the same way or perhaps different ways?

Figure 1.3 depicts a progression from attention to service quality and customer satisfaction to a concern about customer value and the competitive, individual, and high-quality service offered by a performance-based or "customer-driven organization."[21] "A customer-driven organization is defined as one that maintains a focus on the . . . expectations, both spoken and unspoken, of customers, both present and future, in the creation and/or improvement of the . . . service provided."[22]

Susan Rosenblatt argues that the library is no longer "the sole repository of scholarly information; that responsibility rests in a shared, distributed environment including government, private firms, scholarly societies,

FIGURE 1.3
From Service Quality and Satisfaction to Customer "Delight"
(in an Organization Viewing Its Services from the Customer's Perspective)

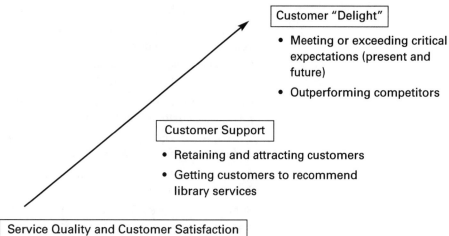

Customer "Delight"
- Meeting or exceeding critical expectations (present and future)
- Outperforming competitors

Customer Support
- Retaining and attracting customers
- Getting customers to recommend library services

Service Quality and Customer Satisfaction
- Delivering what is promised: not raising false expectations
- Providing what customers expect
- Anticipating expectations
- Responding to complaints and problems

various campus departments, university IT services, and libraries." The unfolding twenty-first century will bring new competitors, technologies, and expectations, and the likely continuation of misperceptions such as, "Will the Web offer all or most information and presumably knowledge contained in libraries?," "Can the search engine replace the librarian?," and "Why do we need large warehouses of books if everything can be digitized?"[23] Figure 1.3 is intended as a reminder that customers seek and *value* service organizations that provide better benefits (products, service, and relationships), review and expand the critical expectations that they are willing to meet, outperform their competitors, and offer service at an acceptable cost. Cost need not be defined in monetary terms; it may relate to one's time, for instance.

As a number of books on service quality and customer service indicate, complaints are, in fact, opportunities for improvement and for creating a dialogue with and delighting customers. Berry, who has cataloged common customer-service complaints (see figure 1.4), shows that managers might be able to anticipate customer reactions and to take action before complaints occur. A well-trained and customer-oriented staff is essential for retaining customers while attracting new ones. Aesthetically pleasing library buildings can become social centers providing welcome human contact at a time when technology and the Internet are severing face-to-face interaction, and well-designed Web sites, especially ones that make a full array of services easily available, offer services to customers during the night when many libraries are closed.

FIGURE 1.4
Common Customer-Service Complaints

1. *True lies* Blatant dishonesty or unfairness, such as service providers selling unneeded services or purposely quoting fake, "lowball" cost estimates

2. *Red alert* Providers who assume customers are stupid or dishonest and treat them harshly or disrespectfully

3. *Broken promises* Service providers that do not show up as promised; careless, mistake-prone service

4. *I just work here* Powerless employees who lack authority—or the desire—to solve basic customer problems

5. *The big wait* Waiting in a line made long because some of the checkout lanes or service counters are closed

6. *Automatic pilot* Impersonal, emotionless, no-eye-contact, going-through-the-motions nonservice

7. *Suffering in silence* Employees who do not bother to communicate with customers who are anxious to hear how a service problem will be resolved

8. *Do not ask* Employees unwilling to make any extra effort to help customers, or who seem put out by requests for assistance

9. *Lights on, no one home* Clueless employees who do not know (i.e., will not take the time to learn) the answers to customers' common questions

10. *Misplaced priorities* Employees who visit with each other or conduct personal business while the customer waits; those who refuse to assist a customer because they are off duty or on a break

Adapted with the permission of The Free Press, a Division of Simon & Schuster, from *Discovering the Soul of Service: The Nine Drivers of Sustainable Business Success* by Leonard L. Berry, 3. Copyright © 1999 by Leonard L. Berry.

Web Sources on Customer Service

The World Wide Web offers numerous products, services, and information ranging from text to visuals. Some of the best and most interesting sites are identified as appendix C of Ron Zemke and John A. Woods' *Best Practices in Customer Service*. For example,

CustomerSat.com (http://www.customersat.com) discusses "enhancing customer loyalty" via the Web, "personalizing surveys and invitations," and Internet surveys for measuring satisfaction and for conducting market research.

Customer Value, Inc. (http://www.cval.com), presents "the art and science of measuring customers' needs and wants and finding ways to serve those expectations better than the competition."

The Right Answer Customer Service Finessing Center (http://www.therightanswer.com) of The Right Answer, Inc., has a monthly customer service award, a chat room, training tips, links to customer service Web sites, and other relevant resources.

The American Productivity and Quality Center (http://www.apqc.org/) focuses on best practices, benchmarking, products and services, and discussions of measurement.[24]

Although not listed in the appendix, the National Partnership for Reinventing Government (http://www.npr.gov), a Web maintained by the staff of Vice President Albert Gore Jr., also reports on customer service and best practices in the federal government. A number of the publications and other resources available at this site are relevant to libraries and other nongovernment organizations. These are but a few of the growing and changing resources available on the Web.

Summary

Organizational performance improvement and responsiveness to predetermined customer expectations should match the library's mission and guide the array of services planned and offered. Such improvement and responsiveness also support niche services, those typically associated with research libraries that serve scholars worldwide and strive to be the best in the world. In some cases, librarians place their own spin on service content and delivery to differentiate libraries from most of their competitors. Regardless, whatever services are offered need to embrace the core values of librarianship, to prepare for the challenges of the future, and to demonstrate that the library is essential to the social and educational fabric of the community as well as to the advancement of knowledge and to the economic well-being of the community (via service to business and industry).[25]

Service should be relationship-driven (between the customer and the library), and whatever service is provided comprises the means, not the end. The end relates to what customers gain from service delivery—having their information needs satisfied. Specific services, and the execution of how libraries deliver them, become the library's competitive edge. Organization performance improvement that is attentive to customers, therefore, gives libraries the competitive edge.

Service quality and satisfaction focus on developing and maintaining that customer relationship and that competitive edge. The focus is no longer merely on collections and things that the library possesses; rather, the core activity is the people served and the relationship (ideally a long-term one) between them and the library.

Achieving a dynamic customer relationship requires a vision of service that the library develops, implements, maintains, and adjusts in a changing environment and to meet shifting service expectations. Subsequent chapters explain what comprises service quality and satisfaction, and how to accomplish an ongoing relationship with customers within a planning framework that balances the achievement of the way that libraries do business with the provision of high-quality service and of appropriate tools for staff to do their jobs well.

Put yourself in the customer's shoes and
try to think like the customer.

Since you have lots of interactions with
customers, you should always be on the lookout
for how things can be made better for them.[26]

NOTES

1. Dale S. Montanelli and Patricia F. Stenstrom, eds., *People Come First: User-Centered Academic Library Service* (Chicago: American Library Assn., Assn. of College and Research Libraries, 1999).

2. Irene B. Hoadley, "Reflections: Management Morphology—How We Got to Be Who We Are," *Journal of Academic Librarianship* 25, no. 4 (July 1999): 273.

3. Susan Smith, "How to Create a Plan to Deliver Great Customer Service," in *Best Practices in Customer Service*, eds. Ron Zemke and John A. Woods (New York: AMACOM, 1999), 55.

4. Ibid.

5. See Peter Hernon and Ellen Altman, *Assessing Service Quality: Satisfying the Expectations of Library Customers* (Chicago: American Library Assn., 1998), 1–69; Peter Hernon, Danuta Nitecki, and Ellen Altman, "Service Quality and Customer Satisfaction: An Assessment and Future Directions," *Journal of Academic Librarianship* 25, no. 1 (Jan. 1999): 9–17.

6. Darlene E. Weingand, *Customer Service Excellence: A Concise Guide for Librarians* (Chicago: American Library Assn., 1997), 2, 3.

7. Hoadley, "Reflections: Management Morphology," 269.

8. Suzanne Walters, *Customer Service: A How-to-Do-It Manual for Librarians* (New York: Neal-Schuman, 1994), 3.

9. Bernd Stauss and Christian Friege, "Regaining Service Customers," *Journal of Service Research* 1, no. 4 (May 1999): 350.

10. Susan Rosenblatt, "Information Technology Investments in Research Libraries," *Educom Review* 34, no. 4 (July/Aug. 1999): 44.

11. Brian L. Hawkins, "Distributed Learning and Institutional Restructuring," *Educom Review* 34, no. 4 (July/Aug. 1999): 13.

12. Rosenblatt, "Information Technology Investments in Research Libraries," 45.

13. Ibid., 44.

14. Leonard L. Berry, *Discovering the Soul of Service: The Nine Drivers of Sustainable Business Success* (New York: The Free Press, 1999), 22.

15. Ibid., 23.

16. Weingand, *Customer Service Excellence*, 7, 8.

17. Ibid., 8.

18. Ibid., 9.

19. Hoadley, "Reflections: Management Morphology," 271.

20. See, for instance, Ching-chih Chen and Peter Hernon, *Information-Seeking: Assessing and Anticipating User Needs* (New York: Neal-Schuman, 1982); Cheryl Metoyer-Duran, *Gatekeepers in Ethnolinguistic Communities* (Norwood, N.J.: Ablex, 1993).

21. Morris B. Holbrook, "The Nature of Customer Value: An Axiology of Services in the Consumption Experience," in *Service Quality: New Directions in Theory and Practice*, eds. Roland T. Rust and Richard L. Oliver (Thousand Oaks, Calif.: Sage, 1994), 28, 37.

22. U.S. National Performance Review, *Serving the American Public: Best Practices in Customer-Driven Strategic Planning*, Federal Benchmarking Consortium Study Report (Washington, D.C.: National Performance Review, 1997), 7.

23. Rosenblatt, "Information Technology Investments in Research Libraries," 30, 31.

24. Ron Zemke and John A. Woods, eds., *Best Practices in Customer Service* (New York: AMACOM, 1999), 401–10.

25. Glen E. Holt, Donald Elliott, and Amonia Moore, "Placing a Value on Public Library Services," *Public Libraries* 38, no. 2 (March/April 1999): 98.

26. Both quotations from John R. Whitman, *How to Be an Outstanding Service Employee* (Wellesley, Mass.: Surveytools, 1999), 12. Available: http://www.surveytools.com.

2

Understanding Service Quality

A belief that service is "good enough" does not inspire an organization to improve and challenge itself.

Customers are the greatest asset for any organization.[1]

Various writers have referred to service quality as an antecedent to (or even the same as) satisfaction, whereas some writers (e.g., Jo Ann M. Duffy and Alice A. Ketchand) regard service quality and satisfaction as interrelated, but separate, concepts on a par with each other.[2] Service quality deals with expectations—those specific ones that the library chooses to meet—and satisfaction is more of an emotional and subjective reaction to a time-limited event or the entire experience that one has, over time, with a service provider. Satisfaction, as discussed in chapter 3, also examines expectations, but from a complementary perspective. Furthermore, satisfaction is transaction specific. *Service-encounter satisfaction* is how much a customer likes or dislikes an actual service encounter, whereas *overall service satisfaction* is the customer's feeling of satisfaction or dissatisfaction based on all of that person's experiences with the service organization. Mary Jo Bitner and Amy R. Hubert found that both satisfaction constructs differed from each other and from service quality, thereby reinforcing the assertion of Duffy and Ketchand.[3] Further evidence that satisfaction (and dissatisfaction) are not necessarily directly linked to the service provided might include the following example:

Customers leaving a restaurant or hotel are asked if they were satisfied with the service they received. If they answer "no," we tend to assume service was poor. Direct service providers, such as waitresses, also note that at times the best service efforts are criticized because the customer's perceptions of the service are clouded by being in a bad mood or having a disagreement with someone just before arriving at the restaurant. These service providers recognize that in practice the influence of service quality on customer satisfaction is affected by other factors, one of which is the customers themselves.[4]

As another example, customer dissatisfaction with the library might be due to "an inconvenient parking arrangement rather than poor service delivery. This problem is one that the service employee cannot solve."[5] According to the work of L. M. Aleamoni and of H. W. Marsh, in the case of higher education, the extent of satisfaction might be attributed to the quality of teaching and factors such as student motivation and course level and grade expectations, type of academic field, and workload.[6] Service quality, on the other hand, involves customer expectations of service organizations such as libraries.

This book does not argue against the examination of customer satisfaction. Rather, it encourages librarians to be cautious in attributing causality and to investigate both service quality and satisfaction. Each provides a different part of a picture; together, they reflect the entire picture—from the customer's perspective.

What Is Service Quality?

In library and information science, service quality is typically defined in terms of gap analysis, or the gap between customers' expectations in general (for an ideal library and its services) and those perceptions relating to the particular library and its services. In other words, it is the gap between customer expectations of those services of an academic or public library in general and those perceptions of the services offered by a particular academic or public library. A survey, therefore, might take a set of expectations that any library is willing to meet and then repeat the same set, but this time aimed at a particular academic or public library.

For example, based on the discussion of the planning process in chapter 4 and the service plan in chapter 5, let us assume that the staff of a library consider meeting the following set of customer expectations as their highest priority:

The online catalog

  displays information that is clear and easy to follow

  displays the holdings of school and department libraries

  has easy-to-follow instructions

  indicates the number of copies available

  is an accurate source of information about all material held by the library

  is easily accessible from outside the library building

The Web site

    is attractive

    is easy to navigate

    leads me to the information I am seeking

    enables me to

        interact with library staff

        access a variety of electronic resources

        log on whenever I want

        log on easily

    includes online request forms (e.g., reference and interlibrary loan)

Equipment in good working order is available when I need it. The library provides

    computers dedicated only for online catalog use

    computer printers

    computer workstations (e.g., for access to the Web and electronic texts and journals)

    electronic plugs and network ports (for laptop computers)

    photocopiers

    microfilm/fiche readers

    microfilm/fiche printers

Library staff are

    approachable and welcoming

    available when I need them

    courteous and polite

    friendly and easy to talk to

    expert in

        finding general information

        the literature of my discipline

Materials are

    reshelved promptly

    in their proper places on the shelves

It is easy to browse print collections

It is easy to find where materials are located in the building

The lighting in the building is adequate to meet my needs

Directional signs in the library are

    clear

    helpful

    understandable

It is easy to find out, in advance, when the library is open

I feel safe when using the library

Figure 2.1 takes a number of these expectations and illustrates how to convert them into a questionnaire that measures general expectations and perceptions of the service provided by the particular library. The difference in scores between the two comprises the service gap. In essence, as the gap widens, the extent of a service problem increases. Conversely, the smaller the gap, the more that library services are aligned with customers' expectations. (Chapter 8 explains the rationale behind the ten-point scale.) Figure 2.1 modifies the format of SERVQUAL, a general instrument used in marketing for measuring the service quality gap and for making comparisons of general expectations across service industries. SERVQUAL does not let staff set their own service expectations; it is less flexible than the form presented here. Section B in figure 2.1 links the survey to SERVQUAL; however, many libraries might prefer to delete that section, thereby shortening the length of the form. The features in section B permit a very imprecise comparison with other libraries and service industries. A further complication in making valid comparisons is that librarians may not want to include the appearance of staff in the first statement (section B) and that customers may not understand what "communication materials" are. The term might be either dropped or clarified.

Section C of figure 2.1 pertains to academic libraries. Thus, public libraries might take selected questions from figure 6.2, the customer satisfaction questionnaire, that provide demographic information about respondents. As well, question 6 in section A about library materials would require modification for public libraries. Please remember that the expectations given in figure 2.1 should be reviewed by staff and changed to match local priorities.

Some researchers argue that a survey might omit the set of general expectations (the "in ideal library" in section A of figure 2.1) and contrast perceived expectations for the particular library (customer responses) with staff perceptions about how the service is actually provided.[7] Naturally, evaluators would need some objective measure of service performance. Evaluators might even use focus groups to see how the staff react to survey findings. Or if expectations, for instance, declare a time frame (e.g., "acknowledge you immediately and serve you within five minutes or call additional staff"), evaluators might periodically visit service areas and use a stopwatch to determine the extent to which the library meets the goal of five minutes.

It is also possible for libraries to use the survey in figure 2.1, or a modification of it, to gain a baseline of "ideal" expectations. In subsequent surveys, they might inquire only about expectations of the particular library (minus the portion on "in the ideal library"). Again, they might also omit section B. Clearly, the purpose of figure 2.1 is for the library to gain an overall impression of service quality without having to focus on individual services. Such services, however, could become the subject of an investigation.

In conclusion, libraries should review and revise the expectations and features presented in figure 2.1, settling on those that the library is willing and able to meet. More than likely, whatever decisions are made will address services within the physical building as well as services offered remotely.

FIGURE 2.1
Library Customer Survey

SECTION A

IDEAL LIBRARY Directions: Based on your experiences as a user of library services, please think about the ideal kind of library that would deliver an excellent quality of service. Please indicate the extent to which you think such a library should possess the feature described by each of the statements listed below.

If you feel a feature is "of no importance" for excellent libraries, circle the number **"1"** for **"strongly disagree."**

If you feel a feature is "of highest importance" for excellent libraries, circle **"10"** for **"strongly agree."**

If your feelings are less strong, circle one of the numbers in the middle.

If you have **"no opinion,"** however, please skip the statement.

XXX LIBRARY Directions: The same set of statements relate to your feelings about the services offered by XXX Library. For each statement, please show the extent to which you believe XXX has the feature described by the statement.

Circling a **"1"** means that you **"strongly disagree"** that the library has that feature.

Circling a **"10"** means that you **"strongly agree."**

You may circle any of the numbers in the middle that reflect your feelings.

If you have **"no opinion,"** however, please skip the statement.

There are no right or wrong answers. All we are interested in is the number that truly conveys your feelings regarding excellent service quality in libraries.

SD = strongly disagree

SA = strongly agree

	In Ideal Library	In XXX Library
	SD ⟷ ... SA	SD ⟷ ... SA
1. The online catalog		
a. Displays information that is clear and easy to understand	1 2 3 4 5 6 7 8 9 10	1 2 3 4 5 6 7 8 9 10
b. Has easy-to-follow instructions	1 2 3 4 5 6 7 8 9 10	1 2 3 4 5 6 7 8 9 10
c. Indicates the number of copies available	1 2 3 4 5 6 7 8 9 10	1 2 3 4 5 6 7 8 9 10
d. Is an accurate source of information about all material held by the library	1 2 3 4 5 6 7 8 9 10	1 2 3 4 5 6 7 8 9 10
e. Is easily accessible from outside the library building	1 2 3 4 5 6 7 8 9 10	1 2 3 4 5 6 7 8 9 10
2. The library Web site		
a. Is attractive	1 2 3 4 5 6 7 8 9 10	1 2 3 4 5 6 7 8 9 10
b. Is easy to navigate	1 2 3 4 5 6 7 8 9 10	1 2 3 4 5 6 7 8 9 10
c. Enables me to:		
(1) Access a variety of electronic resources	1 2 3 4 5 6 7 8 9 10	1 2 3 4 5 6 7 8 9 10
(2) Interact with library staff	1 2 3 4 5 6 7 8 9 10	1 2 3 4 5 6 7 8 9 10
(3) Log on easily	1 2 3 4 5 6 7 8 9 10	1 2 3 4 5 6 7 8 9 10
(4) Log on whenever I want	1 2 3 4 5 6 7 8 9 10	1 2 3 4 5 6 7 8 9 10
d. Includes online request forms (reference and interlibrary loan)	1 2 3 4 5 6 7 8 9 10	1 2 3 4 5 6 7 8 9 10

	In Ideal Library	In XXX Library

<table>
<tr><th></th><th colspan="2">In Ideal Library</th><th colspan="2">In XXX Library</th></tr>
<tr><td></td><td>SD</td><td>SA</td><td>SD</td><td>SA</td></tr>
</table>

3. Equipment in good working order is available when I need it. The library provides

  a. Computers dedicated only for online catalog use
    1 2 3 4 5 6 7 8 9 10   1 2 3 4 5 6 7 8 9 10

  b. Computer workstations (for example, for access to the Web, electronic journals, and texts)
    1 2 3 4 5 6 7 8 9 10   1 2 3 4 5 6 7 8 9 10

  c. Computer printers
    1 2 3 4 5 6 7 8 9 10   1 2 3 4 5 6 7 8 9 10

  d. Microform/fiche printers
    1 2 3 4 5 6 7 8 9 10   1 2 3 4 5 6 7 8 9 10

  e. Microform/fiche readers
    1 2 3 4 5 6 7 8 9 10   1 2 3 4 5 6 7 8 9 10

  f. Photocopiers
    1 2 3 4 5 6 7 8 9 10   1 2 3 4 5 6 7 8 9 10

4. The staff are

  a. Approachable and welcoming
    1 2 3 4 5 6 7 8 9 10   1 2 3 4 5 6 7 8 9 10

  b. Available when I need them
    1 2 3 4 5 6 7 8 9 10   1 2 3 4 5 6 7 8 9 10

  c. Courteous and polite
    1 2 3 4 5 6 7 8 9 10   1 2 3 4 5 6 7 8 9 10

  d. Expert in

    (1) Finding general information
    1 2 3 4 5 6 7 8 9 10   1 2 3 4 5 6 7 8 9 10

    (2) The literature of my discipline
    1 2 3 4 5 6 7 8 9 10   1 2 3 4 5 6 7 8 9 10

  e. Friendly and easy to talk to
    1 2 3 4 5 6 7 8 9 10   1 2 3 4 5 6 7 8 9 10

5. The staff provide assistance to help me

  a. Identify resources I need
    1 2 3 4 5 6 7 8 9 10   1 2 3 4 5 6 7 8 9 10

  b. Retrieve resources I need
    1 2 3 4 5 6 7 8 9 10   1 2 3 4 5 6 7 8 9 10

  c. Evaluate information I find
    1 2 3 4 5 6 7 8 9 10   1 2 3 4 5 6 7 8 9 10

  d. Learn how to find information
    1 2 3 4 5 6 7 8 9 10   1 2 3 4 5 6 7 8 9 10

6. Library materials

  a. Encompass curriculum-supporting videos and films
    1 2 3 4 5 6 7 8 9 10   1 2 3 4 5 6 7 8 9 10

  b. Meet my course/research needs
    1 2 3 4 5 6 7 8 9 10   1 2 3 4 5 6 7 8 9 10

7. When I request materials, I am told how long they will take to arrive

  a. From restricted collections
    1 2 3 4 5 6 7 8 9 10   1 2 3 4 5 6 7 8 9 10

  b. Through interlibrary loan
    1 2 3 4 5 6 7 8 9 10   1 2 3 4 5 6 7 8 9 10

8. Materials are

  a. In their proper places on the shelves
    1 2 3 4 5 6 7 8 9 10   1 2 3 4 5 6 7 8 9 10

  b. Reshelved promptly
    1 2 3 4 5 6 7 8 9 10   1 2 3 4 5 6 7 8 9 10

9. It is easy to

  a. Browse print collections
    1 2 3 4 5 6 7 8 9 10   1 2 3 4 5 6 7 8 9 10

  b. Find where materials are located in the building
    1 2 3 4 5 6 7 8 9 10   1 2 3 4 5 6 7 8 9 10

(continued)

FIGURE 2.1
Library Customer Survey (continued)

	In Ideal Library	In XXX Library
	SD SA	SD SA
10. Directional signs are clear and helpful	1 2 3 4 5 6 7 8 9 10	1 2 3 4 5 6 7 8 9 10
11. It is easy to find out, in advance, when the library is open	1 2 3 4 5 6 7 8 9 10	1 2 3 4 5 6 7 8 9 10
12. Other expectations you consider important		
a. _____	1 2 3 4 5 6 7 8 9 10	1 2 3 4 5 6 7 8 9 10
b. _____	1 2 3 4 5 6 7 8 9 10	1 2 3 4 5 6 7 8 9 10
c. _____	1 2 3 4 5 6 7 8 9 10	1 2 3 4 5 6 7 8 9 10

SECTION B

Directions: Listed below are *five* features of libraries and the services they offer. We would like to know how important each of these features is to you when you evaluate a library's quality of service. Please assign a total of 100 points among the five features according to how important each feature is to you. The more important a feature is to you, the more points you should assign to it. Please make sure that the points you give to the five features add up to 100.

1. The appearance of the library's physical facilities, equipment, personnel, and communication materials.   _____ points

2. The library's ability to perform promised services dependably and accurately.   _____ points

3. The library's willingness to help readers and provide prompt services.   _____ points

4. The knowledge and courtesy of the library staff and their ability to inspire trust and confidence.   _____ points

5. The caring, individualized attention the library provides to its readers.   _____ points

                                   TOTAL points allocated   100   points

6. Which *one* feature among the above five is *most* important to you? (Circle your choice)   1 2 3 4 5

7. Which *one* feature among the above five is *least* important to you? (Circle your choice)   1 2 3 4 5

8. Is there anything else not included in these five features that you find important in evaluating the quality of service you receive?

_____ Yes Please specify _____

_____ No

SECTION C

Directions: Please answer a few more questions for us.

1. Overall, to what extent does the service that XXX Library provides meet your expectations for an excellent library?

Falls Short   **Meets**   **Surpasses**

        −3   −2   −1   0   +1   +2   +3

2. Specifically, does any XXX Library department or service merit a ranking of less than +3 on the above scale?

_____ Yes   _____ No

If "yes," which one(s)? _____

Why? _____

_____

_____

_____

_____

_____

3. Please estimate how many times you have used XXX Library during this school term.

a. _____ Daily   d. _____ Less than once a week

b. _____ Several times a week   e. _____ Other (please specify): _____

c. _____ Once a week   _____

4. What best describes you?

a. _____ Undergraduate student   d. _____ Staff

b. _____ Graduate student   e. _____ Other (please specify): _____

c. _____ Faculty   _____

5. What general category best describes your discipline?

a. _____ Behavioral sciences   e. _____ Social sciences

b. _____ Humanities   f. _____ Undecided

c. _____ Medical sciences   g. _____ Other (please specify): _____

d. _____ Physical sciences   _____

Thank you very much for participating in this study.

*Adapted from Danuta Nitecki and Peter Hernon, "Measuring Service Quality at Yale University's Libraries," *Journal of Academic Librarianship* 26 (July 2000): 259–73.

Shifting Expectations

It seems logical to assume that customer expectations about library services will be influenced by the use of other service providers. For example, overnight package carriers, such as FedEx and United Parcel Service, emphasize speedy and accurate delivery. Students often regard the World Wide Web as providing rapid access to information. Thus, one might hypothesize that more library customers will seek speedy and prompt service from libraries (e.g., for document delivery). They will also be dissatisfied with slow response times from library computers.

A number of bookstores encourage browsing and reading and operate cafés so that customers can combine reading with leisure, food, and drink. Thus, customers may have some bookstore and café expectations of a library. Finally, as more college students study late at night or in the early morning hours, they may require or perhaps demand remote access to appropriate library materials at these nontraditional service times. Remote access to library resources may need to address this situation and the potential problems encountered in customers' accessing and retrieving information.

Thus, libraries might monitor other service providers to see what expectations libraries should try to meet or exceed when revising and refining their service reputation to ensure that they fulfill their mission statement by concentrating on those expectations important to their customers. On the other hand, while reviewing other service providers, libraries might encounter providers that they can regularly outperform. They might also encounter instances of bad service that have negative implications for the organization's service reputation. As the following example illustrates, problems can arise when staff are poorly trained. One (unnamed) telephone carrier claims to have more than 150 service plans but apparently does not ask for permission regularly to review customers' use patterns and to recommend adjustments in the service plans held. More importantly, this carrier has customer service representatives who are often poorly trained. As an unobtrusive project, one of the authors of this book called the service department of this carrier and asked for the specifics about the plan his family had. There was great variation in what the carrier claimed were the actual provisions of the plan, and these differences had significant cost implications. Apparently, with each phone call, the representative entered a notation in the record that the customer had made an inquiry, but at no point did an extensive number of inquiries trigger a call from a supervisor or other personnel. It would seem that this carrier is satisfied with the status quo, and it would probably take a significant financial loss for change to occur. Clearly, the upper-level administration of this carrier is either unaware of the situation or uninterested in change—satisfied with the present level of profit.

Libraries might be unwilling to publicize that they outperformed specific companies. Regardless, the information might further motivate staff and might be shared informally with those to whom the library director reports.

Data Collection

Multiple methods of data collection produce more in-depth insights and encourage staff to become more data-conscious. Thus, a service quality survey may be important but should not be the sole method of data collection. For example, the University of Phoenix wants to be the "leader in adult education" and to do this "means to gather salient information continuously, and to use the enormous amount of data as quickly as possible. We are accountable, each day, to . . . students, faculty and shareholders." The university conducts ten major surveys on a continuous basis:

registration survey	comments to department chair
student end-of-course survey	exit survey
faculty end-of course survey	faculty involvement survey
graduation survey	alumni survey
internal customer (staff) survey	employer survey

In addition, the university has a comprehensive student cognition assessment, which it first administers at the time of admission; an affective assessment, which "assesses the development and change of personal and professional values, attitudes, and self-reported behaviors known or believed to be relevant to success in professional disciplines"; a communication skills inventory of "a student's written, oral, and group communication and presentation skills"; a portfolio assessment, which monitors "a student's professional and personal development"; a critical thinking assessment; and an external validation, which examines cognitive skills and critical thinking.[8]

The university tracks students from admission to graduation and gathers information from past students and employers. The university's Department of Institutional Research has built the assessment process into the fabric of the institution. Clearly, most academic and public libraries, and their broader institutions or organizations, rarely demonstrate the same commitment to assessment. Nonetheless, libraries have choices about what they assess. The choices may include information about customers' perceptions about their service and learning expectations and their degree of satisfaction with the services provided.

Libraries have choices about what types of data collection they use. As *Assessing Service Quality* illustrates, evaluation does not necessarily require the use of self-reporting questionnaires and formal investigation.[9] Libraries might even combine surveys with informal means, as long as they are unconcerned about return rates and generalization from a sample to a known population. Libraries, for example, might leave stacks of questionnaires (formatted as comment cards typically found in hotels and restaurants) in a prominent location for interested customers to pick up and complete at their convenience.

As discussed in depth in chapter 7, libraries might also use e-mail and the World Wide Web, including their home pages, to survey customers and to gain insights into service quality and satisfaction. John Chisholm offers an important reminder:

Without the assurance of confidentiality, many customers will not respond candidly, or perhaps at all. In a confidential survey, a response may be linked to a customer name, but only by a survey researcher for purposes of survey management. An anonymous survey goes further: a response cannot be linked to a customer name at all.[10]

Commitment to "World-Class" Service Quality

Ongoing attention to service quality and satisfaction requires a well-trained staff that feels empowered and regards customer service as the highest priority of the organization. At the same time, there must be "genuine passion for delighting customers throughout the entire organization" within the context of those expectations that the library is willing to accept as highest priority.[11] Furthermore, "if an organization truly wants to encourage world-class performance, it must provide appropriate rewards."[12] A reward might be recognition—public praise of a staff member or a team—at an appropriate ceremony.

Marla Royne Stafford has taken these threads of service quality and woven them together into "a normative model for improving service quality" that can be adapted to nonprofit organizations. That model, as adapted in figure 2.2, contains ten stages for continuous quality improvement. As Stafford explains, "one stage does not simply flow into the next. Rather, there is an intertwining of various stages with one leading into another and back." Stafford's ten stages are

1. *Management commitment* Management must become committed to quality improvement and communicate that to employees.

2. *Employee commitment and participation* Employees must become committed to the program and participate fully in the process.

3. *Employee education and training* Employees must be taught their role in quality improvement as well as learn each stage of the program.

4. *Employee communication* Communication channels must be established and utilized to ensure a constant and appropriate information flow between employees and management.

5. *Internal organization* A quality director should be selected, and individuals should be assigned their quality improvement responsibilities.

6. *Documentation and objective setting* Each employee should set personal quality-improvement objectives, both qualitative and quantitative, that conform to library policies and expectations.

7. *Assessment and modification processes* An evaluation of current quality levels must be performed, and modifications to existing procedures should be developed and implemented.

8. *Outcomes and targets*   Controls should be established to ensure continued and successful change.
9. *Integration*   The stages should be merged together to ensure a smoothly operating system.
10. *Continuation*   Quality improvement is a continuous process.[13]

Stages 5 and 6, for instance, should be adjusted for libraries to ensure that management and staff at all levels of the organization support the customer plan, pledge, and any other organizational promises. All units of the library should work to accomplish customer-based goals, objectives, outcomes, and targets. Any personal objectives that individual staff set should be in line with the direction in which the organization is going.

FIGURE 2.2
Model for Improving Service Quality

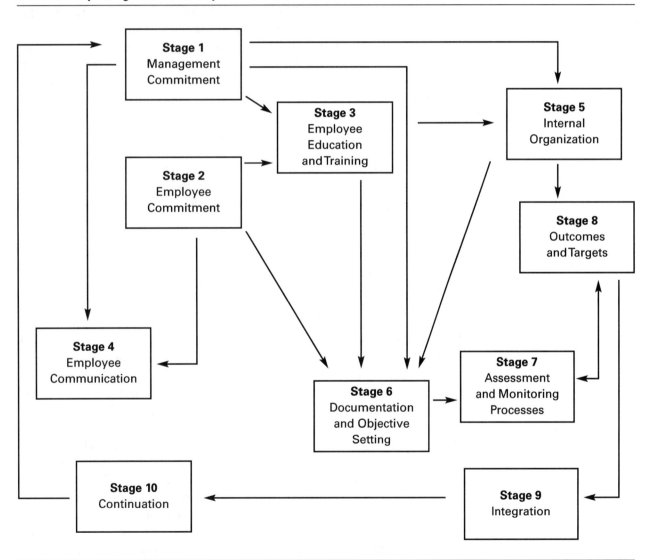

Adapted from Marla Royne Stafford, "A Normative Model for Improving Services Quality," *Journal of Customer Services in Marketing & Management* 1, no. 1 (1994): 18.

As figure 2.2 illustrates, the organization must pay attention to service quality on a continuous basis. Both management and staff must make a commitment to it as service becomes the central focus of the library. Clearly, the staff will require education and training on service improvement, and all staff—regardless of department—must see where service fits into what they do. Together, the staff and management set the assessment framework together, and they monitor the extent to which the organization meets objectives, outcomes, and targets.

Library Centrality

In *Academic Library Centrality*, Deborah J. Grimes argues that the academic library has lost its position as the "heart" of the college, university, or institution of higher education. By extension, the public library is often not the heart or pulse of the community. She notes the academic library's decrease in the share of institutional funding and maintains that the library can become central to the institution and contribute "to the university's mission, and, subsequently, how it accrues the power necessary to acquire resources that support its programs and activities."[14] By extension, the same applies to college and public libraries.

Grimes equates library centrality with regaining power, achieving "user success," and ensuring an "agile organization . . . [that confronts] the specter of obsolescence or failure to meet user needs and address[es] specific weaknesses within the library."[15] She views *user success* (in achieving overall educational success), the operational definition of library centrality, in terms of three indicators: service, access, and tradition. Figure 2.3 depicts centrality for the academic library; presumably, a number of the characteristics or indicators apply to public libraries as well. "User" opinion and satisfaction surveys may also be applied to a number of the indicators specified for service, access, and tradition. Nonetheless, Grimes believes that

> User success seems to provide a better focus for academic library performance than user satisfaction, which, when called customer satisfaction, is the pivotal concern of the total quality management (TQM) movement now in vogue in many academic institutions, including academic libraries. A focus on satisfaction alone seems to overlook the primary mission of the educational institution—which is to educate. The student is more than a customer in educational institutions; he or she is also the product of the institution. A customer, for example, merely purchases or buys a product or service. Education, by definition, is more than this: It is "the act or process of imparting or acquiring general knowledge and of developing the powers of reasoning and judgment." The student does more than "buy" an educational service; the student receives something from the university (i.e., an education) and then *becomes* something more as a result (i.e., an individual with greater knowledge and better-developed powers of reasoning and judgment). Consequently, user success is a more complex concept than user satisfaction, . . . [and it is] appropriate to the more complex customer-product relationship of a university student to the institution.[16]

FIGURE 2.3
Academic Library Centrality

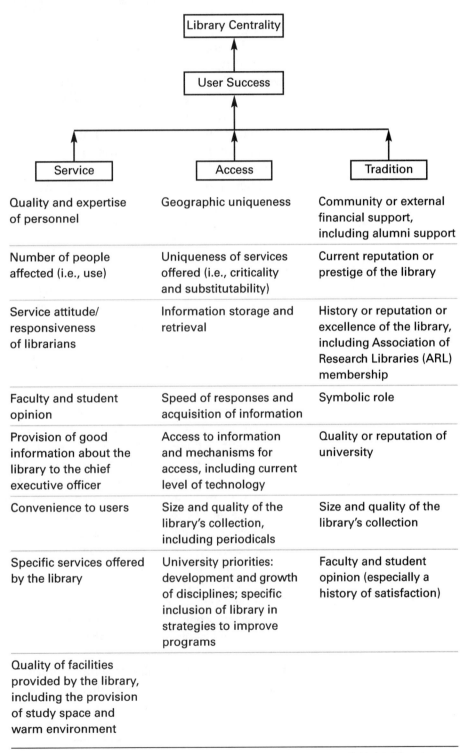

Service	Access	Tradition
Quality and expertise of personnel	Geographic uniqueness	Community or external financial support, including alumni support
Number of people affected (i.e., use)	Uniqueness of services offered (i.e., criticality and substitutability)	Current reputation or prestige of the library
Service attitude/ responsiveness of librarians	Information storage and retrieval	History or reputation or excellence of the library, including Association of Research Libraries (ARL) membership
Faculty and student opinion	Speed of responses and acquisition of information	Symbolic role
Provision of good information about the library to the chief executive officer	Access to information and mechanisms for access, including current level of technology	Quality or reputation of university
Convenience to users	Size and quality of the library's collection, including periodicals	Size and quality of the library's collection
Specific services offered by the library	University priorities: development and growth of disciplines; specific inclusion of library in strategies to improve programs	Faculty and student opinion (especially a history of satisfaction)
Quality of facilities provided by the library, including the provision of study space and warm environment		

Adapted from Deborah J. Grimes, *Academic Library Centrality: User Success through Service, Access, and Tradition* (Chicago: American Library Assn., Assn. of College and Research Libraries, 1998), 105, 109, 110.

Such a characterization of user success, in the minds of students and a number of faculty, applies to the classroom and not so much to the library. Users, or customers, of an academic or public library, as a generalization, prefer to be self-sufficient or self-reliant. They may even avoid or discount the value of library instruction.[17]

In developing her model, Grimes does not refer to the literature on service quality and the fact that service quality applies to *information content, service environment,* and *staff.* Service quality examines the organization from the customer's perspective and what is important to users. Collections become a type of service and, for the public and academic library of today and tomorrow, collections may not be locally held or accessible only at the library: Libraries purchase, lease, or rent databases and resources that customers access remotely.

There is overlap between the indicators of centrality and service quality, but service quality offers libraries a wider range of indicators from which to choose. Nonetheless, those indicators identified in figure 2.3, which customers could legitimately comment on, might be included in any service quality or satisfaction survey that the library adopts—as long as the indicators are important to a library's customers.

Clearly, for various reasons, the metaphor "the heart of the university" no longer applies. A more appropriate metaphor, as Grimes declares, is that of "crossroads community."

> A *crossroads* is defined as "the point at which a vital decision is made" and "a main center of activity or assembly." Initially, the image conjured up by "crossroads" may be that of small rural communities connected by county roads or older state highway systems. Such communities may consist only of gas stations and country stores (now sporting video rentals and tanning booths). Sometimes there are churches and sometimes, depending on the part of the country, there are old, now unused silos and cotton gins and railway stations. At the same time, this humble image is not the only one that can be conjured up with the words "crossroads community." The "community" part of the phrase implies connections, services, people, and resources. . . . The sense of community evident in "crossroads community" adds a warm, human element to the image, saying much about relationships among those who form the community. . . .
>
> The academic library is a scholarly "crossroads community," affected by and affecting its environment, its technology, and its users. Just as a crossroads connects people to other places and other resources, the academic library connects students and faculty to other institutions and information sources.[18]

The metaphor even applies to public libraries and the service responses (see chapter 4) that they choose to fill.

Summary

Delivering excellent service requires that libraries continually receive feedback from customers and promptly respond to those expectations they can legitimately meet. Because service quality is a multifaceted concept that views collections as a type of service and staff, resources, and facilities as supporting services, attention to service quality is definitely not confined to public-service activities. "Service quality, as judged by customers, does not separate the contributions of the product from that of the service given, but, rather, it calls for a more holistic view of what libraries do and how customers perceive their collections."[19] Furthermore, service quality involves recognition of the importance of narrowing the gap between perceptions of services that libraries, in general, should offer and those provided by a particular library. As Thomas A. Childers and Nancy Van House note, libraries are service organizations in which customers are participants "in the face-to-face service transactions and in self-service. . . . Advances in information technology are increasing the range of activities that users can perform for themselves."[20] Thus, in an electronic information age that caters to a more visually oriented, nonprint-oriented population, more libraries will embrace service quality as they face a scarcity of resources and increased competition and as they strive to serve better their customers while simultaneously trying to attract new ones.

Library use is largely self-service.[21]

NOTES

1. Both quotations from Ellen Altman and Peter Hernon, "Service Quality and Customer Satisfaction Do Matter," *American Libraries* 29, no. 7 (Aug. 1998): 54.

2. Jo Ann M. Duffy and Alice A. Ketchand, "Examining the Role of Service Quality in Overall Service Satisfaction," *Journal of Managerial Issues* 10, no. 2 (summer 1998): 240.

3. Mary Jo Bitner and Amy R. Hubert, "Encounter Satisfaction versus Overall Satisfaction versus Quality," in *Service Quality: New Directions in Theory and Practice*, eds. Roland T. Rust and Richard L. Oliver (Thousand Oaks, Calif.: Sage, 1994), 72–94.

4. Duffy and Ketchand, "Examining the Role of Service Quality," 240.

5. Ibid., 246.

6. L. M. Aleamoni, "Student Ratings of Instruction," in *Handbook of Teacher Evaluation*, ed. J. Millman (Beverly Hills, Calif.: Sage, 1981), 110–45; H. W. Marsh, "Students' Evaluations of University Teaching: Research Findings, Methodological Issues, and Directions for Future Research," *International Journal of Educational Research* 11 (1987): 253–88; H. W. Marsh, "Students' Evaluations of University Teaching: Dimensionality, Reliability, Validity, Potential Biases and Utility," *Journal of Educational Psychology* 76 (1984): 707–54.

7. Peter Hernon, Danuta Nitecki, and Ellen Altman, "Service Quality and Customer Satisfaction: An Assessment and Future Directions," *Journal of Academic Librarianship* 25, no. 1 (Jan. 1999): 14–15.

8. University of Phoenix, Department of Institutional Research, "Assessment Systems for Measuring Student Achievement and Improving Institutional Effectiveness" (Phoenix, Ariz.: the University, n.d.). (Brochure.)

9. Peter Hernon and Ellen Altman, *Assessing Service Quality: Satisfying the Expectations of Library Customers* (Chicago: American Library Assn., 1998), 51–5, 79–178.

10. John Chisholm, "Using the Internet to Measure Customer Satisfaction and Loyalty," in *Best Practices in Customer Service*, eds. Ron Zemke and John A. Woods (New York: American Management Assn., 1999), 311.

11. Zemke and Woods, *Best Practices in Customer Service*, 35.

12. Ibid., 36.

13. Marla Royne Stafford, "A Normative Model for Improving Services Quality," *Journal of Customer Services in Marketing & Management* 1, no. 1 (1994): 17, 19.

14. Deborah J. Grimes, *Academic Library Centrality: User Success through Service, Access, and Tradition* (Chicago: American Library Assn., Assn. of College and Research Libraries, 1998), 3.

15. Ibid., 112.

16. Ibid., 112–13.

17. Ellen Altman and Peter Hernon, eds., "Student and Faculty Perceptions about Misconduct: A Case Study," in *Research Misconduct: Issues, Implications, and Strategies* (Greenwich, Conn.: Ablex, 1997), 59–70.

18. Grimes, *Academic Library Centrality*, 118, 119.

19. Hernon, Nitecki, and Altman, "Service Quality and Customer Satisfaction," 10.

20. Thomas A. Childers and Nancy A. Van House, *What's Good? Describing Your Public Library's Effectiveness* (Chicago: American Library Assn., 1993), 27.

21. Ibid., 26.

3

Understanding
Customer Satisfaction

Satisfaction, or lack of it, is the difference between how a customer expects *to be treated, and how he or she* perceives *being treated.*[1]

Service quality and customer satisfaction are not the same. Each are co-equal concepts, and a study of service quality does not necessarily involve an assessment of customer satisfaction or vice versa. Service quality as a *strategic planning tool* denotes the attributes of what a library should be, in the minds of its customers, and the expectations the library regards as essential to meet. The typical means of measuring service quality is called *gap analysis*. Gap analysis may involve a two-step process in which library users are first asked to characterize the attributes of an ideal, or expected, library and are then asked to assess the particular library at hand according to the same dimensions. What is of interest is the degree to which the two assessments produce results meaningful for guiding the provision of customer service. The results are used to measure compliance with a service plan and pledge, as a means of determining how an existing mission—or elements of its execution plan—might be revised, and as a basis on which to develop and refine services in the future.

In contrast, assessing customer satisfaction is a *diagnostic tool*. Customer satisfaction is a measure of how the customer perceives service delivery and possible shortcomings at a particular time. *Overall satisfaction*, which is a general measure, is rated in combination with a limited number of specific service dimensions considered important to gauge at the time of the assessment. (These specific dimensions are a subset of the larger list of dimensions that comprise library service.) The customer satisfaction measurement process includes an opportunity for customers to indicate areas that may require managerial intervention. In this sense, the customer satisfaction assessment is like taking the temperature and blood pressure of a patient, as distinct from conducting an extensive workup involving most, if not all, vital signs. Measuring customer satisfaction can be extremely important as a management tool and can be easily and inexpensively employed. As will be discussed in chapter 5, regardless of whatever other type of surveys the library may undertake, a customer satisfaction survey—as prescribed in this book—is advised every one to two years.

This chapter examines customer satisfaction and explores how it is an important and measurable perception among both library customers and library staff. The chapter reviews what satisfaction is, and how it relates to expectations; how libraries can shift from a transaction relationship to a satisfaction relationship; why it makes sense to segment customers when measuring satisfaction; and why staff should be included in the process.

What Is Satisfaction?

Simply put, satisfaction is a sense of contentment that arises from an *actual* experience in relation to an *expected* experience. The necessary a priori ingredient in satisfaction is the concept of expectations. The degree to which expectations conform to or deviate from experience is the pivotal determinant of satisfaction. The importance of expectations in defining satisfaction merits a close and focused examination, as understanding expectations and the ability to set expectations are crucial to the delivery of service satisfaction.

Service quality also looks at actual versus expected experience, but the focus of service quality is to compare objectively what one wishes as an idealized service attribute with the current condition of that attribute. The process of making such a comparison involves an objective comparison between an ideal possibility and its present reality. By contrast, customer satisfaction measures a customer's immediate and subjective experience with a specific service encounter—a uniquely personal and internalized experience that generates a spontaneous perception based, consciously or subconsciously, on expectations.

It is instructive to distinguish between the following two concepts: actual experience and expected experience. Actual experience is what one perceives in a given momentary situation, whereas expected experience is what one anticipates prior to entering a given situation. Actual experience refers to a highly temporal service event that can influence how one feels generally about service delivery. Understanding how expected experiences are formed provides insights into how to manage the process of setting expectations better.

Figure 3.1, the expectations kernel, illustrates three types of expectations that play a role in determining whether customers find an actual experience satisfying. At the core, expectations can involve elements that may be assumed to be common to all people and that exist (or through proper upbringing become embedded) consciously or unconsciously from birth. Such elements include common courtesy, respect, dignity, and other attributes that make human interaction civilized. These elements are so basic and universal that it is truly shocking when they are violated. Unfortunately, these core expectations can too easily be violated in delivering customer service.

Surrounding this core of expectations are *learned expectations*. Learned expectations are those developed from experience and a widening exposure to the world. As innovative service providers move to offer optional or extra services as part of their core services, people's expectations expand accordingly. What was once an "extra" is now expected as part of a basic package. The reverse can also appear true and is tolerated only if the total experience proves at least as satisfying as before. For example, decades ago in the United States one never had to leave one's car to fill it up with gasoline. A "service attendant" ran out to greet the driver, take the order, and perform a panoply of extra services with alacrity. While the tank was filling, the attendant ran around the car checking the oil level, cleaning the front and rear windows, and sometimes checking the tire pressure and polishing the hubcaps. If the attendant was particularly good, and the driver was of generous mood, the attendant received a tip, which invariably brought a great smile and a genuine "Thank you!" followed by a salute as the driver pulled away. Today, the driver can choose between waiting for an attendant (if such service is available) and paying a premium for the gas and filling the tank

FIGURE 3.1
The Expectations Kernel

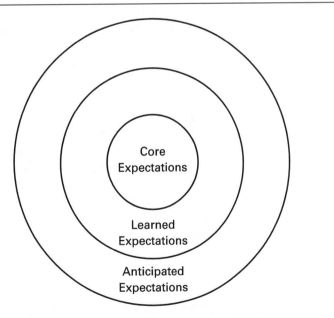

oneself, usually paying slightly less per gallon. Many people now find it preferable simply to serve themselves and be on their way, probably because people today seem in a greater hurry than in decades past and gasoline is more expensive. The trade-off between extra services offered and time and money saved seems demonstrably in favor of the latter option.

In addition to these core and learned expectations is a class of anticipated expectations that come into play when one imagines that a dimension of the experience should be provided, whether it is offered or not. This is most interesting because it means that customers may anticipate a quality of service that is not currently offered. Herein lies a competitive opportunity. The service provider that anticipates these expectations, and offers them before the competition follows suit, not only exceeds customer expectations but contributes to creating a new set of learned expectations, raising the bar for similar service providers. Until these expectations become commonly expected, this astute service provider has a competitive advantage that will likely result in attracting more customers and retaining existing ones.

These three layers of expectations comprise the *expected* experience. Given the relationship between actual experience and expected experience, how does satisfaction take place? When actual experience *meets* one's expectations, the customer is content, and when actual experience *exceeds* expectations, the customer is delighted.

The qualities of contentment and delight are measured in degrees of satisfaction. Difficult to measure objectively, these degrees of satisfaction can be estimated using a subjective assessment process in which the customer is simply asked how satisfied he or she is. This assessment is made possible through the use of a scale on which a customer records the degree of perceived satisfaction on a range from 1, meaning "completely dissatisfied," to 10, meaning "completely satisfied." (See chapter 8 for further discussion of point scales used in surveys.)

In addition to the satisfaction scale, an expectations scale is also used. This scale lets the customer indicate the degree to which his or her expectations were met, were not met, or were exceeded. For example, a seven-point expectations scale might use zero (0) as a midpoint, signifying that expectations were exactly met, and the numbers +1, +2, and +3 extending to the right of the 0 to mean that expectations were exceeded by these degrees, while the numbers –1, –2, and –3 extending to the left of the 0 denote the degree to which expectations were not met. As will be discussed in chapter 6, these two scales, satisfaction and expectations, provide a clear way to see the relationship between these two interconnected concepts.

These scales do not provide an objective measure of satisfaction and expectations. For the purposes of measuring satisfaction, however, customers are likely to report what they consider important. In this sense, the truth is the *perception* that they wish to report, and that is what is important to measure. Perceptions are the key subject in the approach to creating and measuring satisfaction because customer perceptions are the target of influence, and the customer is the most authoritative source to describe these perceptions.

The extent of one's satisfaction is based on ingrained sensibilities, perhaps years of experience, and a broad exposure to innovative service delivery. Together these factors combine to form a solid set of core, learned, and expected expectations. Most definitely, one's perception of satisfaction with any particular service provider can be quite fragile.

No matter how robust one's set of expectations, satisfaction can easily be tilted by a single negative (or positive) encounter. For example, suppose a customer patronizes a particular restaurant for years, being generally quite satisfied with the experience. Then, during one visit, the customer is outraged by the waiter's clumsy spillage of a drink in the customer's lap and the management's subsequent refusal to pay for dry cleaning. This single incident will loom large in the customer's memory, clouding years of otherwise consistent satisfaction.

David B. Pillemer, professor of psychology at Wellesley College, has found that momentous events can color one's memory despite a positive experience over a long period of time. His thesis concerns a life history that "is constructed by connecting time periods surrounding momentous events into a coherent story."[2] A life history seems reasonable if it is applied to any life experience, including experience with the library. So while the concern is with measuring perceived satisfaction, one must be aware that satisfaction is not necessarily a persistent state and can easily change quite suddenly and to a dramatic degree based, perhaps, on a single encounter. This, of course, can be either positive or negative. Either way, it means that the overall satisfaction score can easily and quickly change. Using this information to advantage means delivering consistently acceptable service (meeting expectations) while adding an occasional spike in performance delivered individually to customers, where the spike means providing an unexpected and satisfying experience (exceeding expectations).

A certain number of customers will say that they are satisfied. Paradoxically, that is not the most important or even the most useful finding to emerge from a satisfaction study. What is more useful is to identify how many customers say they are not satisfied and why they are not. In fact, customers who are least satisfied may provide more important feedback than those who are most satisfied. The reason for this curious twist is that already-satisfied customers have little to report on how things can be improved, while if the cause of dissatisfaction among the others can be discovered, and if something is done about it, the overall level of satisfaction might subsequently rise.

For the purposes of clarification, it is useful to look at two types of dissatisfied customers. The first type consists of customers who seem to be chronic complainers. It seems nothing can be done to satisfy them because their expectations are beyond reach. To use an example of a dry-cleaning store, these are the customers that the store's owner will gladly introduce to the competition. And, with a successful introduction to the competition down the street or across town, the once-plagued store will see its profits rise, its morale improve, and its staff turnover reduced. To the extent that the library does not have such options for redirecting undesirable customers, a certain element of disgruntlement may come to be expected, and its presence should be handled sensitively and diplomatically.

Another type of dissatisfied customer is the earnest and sometimes "overqualified" expert who considers it imperative to report how much better things would be if only done the way this person suggests. Although the first inclination may be to dismiss such respondents as complainers, it can take only one astute person to bring attention to a problem that may affect many others who have neglected to point it out or who, in their complaints, have not identified the root cause. The first, and understandable, reaction to criticism is to be defensive. Nonetheless, listening to and resolving the complaints of the most dissatisfied customers are likely to improve the situation for everyone. In any case, such criticisms need not be taken as a personal affront but should be welcomed as an earnest effort on the part of the customer to improve the library.

Shifting to a Satisfaction Relationship

The recommended approach to creating and measuring satisfaction in libraries is a direct outgrowth of work undertaken by Surveytools Corporation for private sector businesses.[3] This approach, however, also applies to libraries and museums as they shift from a transaction relationship to a customer relationship. Following a review of how those relationships are described in a business context, this section proposes a plan for making a similar transformation in libraries.

When a customer patronizes a business such as the corner market, that customer does not give much thought to his or her relationship with the market; he or she simply goes about collecting the needed products, paying for them, and departing. This is probably typical, whether buying food, clothing, garden items, hardware, or other products or services that are needed on a regular or occasional basis. Figure 3.2 illustrates the *transaction relationship*, which shows the simple transaction of service for payment. The business provides a service in exchange for payment by the customer. Each such exchange takes place on a transaction-by-transaction basis. There is no implied or expected ongoing relationship between the business and the customer or vice versa. This relationship between the business (and its employees) and each customer is highly tentative and tenuous, and it will

FIGURE 3.2
The Transaction Relationship

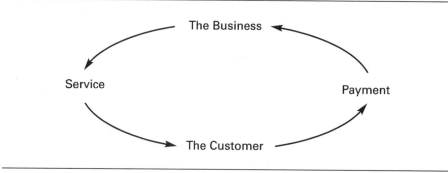

continue until one day, for some reason, the customers go someplace else or the business folds.

It is possible to build a much more explicit and mutually engaging relationship between the customer and the business, in which the business sets specific expectations for service delivery in the mind of the customer and asks the customer, in return, to rate how the business is doing. By engaging the customer in this dialog, a relationship is formed, one in which the customer becomes more aware of and committed to patronizing and improving the business. Figure 3.3 illustrates the new *satisfaction relationship* between the customer and the business. The business provides an explicit set of expectations for the customer, backed up with a satisfaction guarantee. In exchange, the business asks the customer to provide a score that indicates his or her level of satisfaction, along with suggestions for improvement. This relationship goes beyond a mere sales transaction. It puts out front the commitment to satisfy the customer on an ongoing basis and provides a simple way for the customer to report exactly what can be done to keep his or her business.

A central element in maintaining an effective relationship is the process of collecting customer satisfaction data, which gives management far greater control over the relationship than is allowed in the simple transaction relationship: "Running your business without customer satisfaction data is like operating without an accounting system."[4]

The satisfaction relationship can be applied to libraries. It includes

the process of understanding customer expectations, in terms of both service quality and satisfaction

the importance of setting explicit expectations in the minds of customers

delivering service in a way that is enforced by a guarantee to the customer

asking the customer to play an active role in providing the feedback necessary to know how the library is doing and how it can improve, thus further enhancing the relationship between the customer and the library

FIGURE 3.3
The Satisfaction Relationship

Satisfaction and Segmenting

Because not all customers are the same, they should be segmented according to similar characteristics that can have a direct bearing on their expectations and, therefore, on their satisfaction. There are several ways to segment the customer base; obvious ways include segmentation based on gender and age. It is possible for libraries to use U.S. census data to create maps of communities that display demographic distributions based on age, gender, income, race, etc. It is also possible to display data for predetermined variables on a map produced using a geographic information system.[5] These characteristics may not, however, be the most productive ways to segment customers in order to understand satisfaction with library services.

A more relevant basis for segmentation is according to *how* the facility is used. Such information may be gained only from an appropriately designed questionnaire. One group may use the facility as a resource for preschool children, while another group may be interested primarily, and perhaps solely, in reading newspapers and current periodicals. Using these two groups as an example, it becomes clear that they visit entirely separate sections of a public library, are concerned with entirely different materials, may frequent the library at entirely different times of the day and week, and their needs for assistance require entirely different knowledge and perhaps temperament—one oriented to a juvenile customer, the other to a mature and possibly senior customer.[6]

Unless care is taken to measure satisfaction in a way that can differentiate between customer groups, or segments, it is easy to misunderstand how to satisfy these groups, as what is required to satisfy each group may be quite different. A survey questionnaire can reveal how a customer base is segmented and how the various segments perceive whether their expectations are being met. It is critical, however, to include in the questionnaire one or more questions that ask customers to indicate in which segment they belong. Once the survey is completed, it will then be easy to examine exactly how the different groups respond to the same questions, and this will provide insight into how better to respond to their varying needs in appropriate ways. Therefore, before conducting a survey the library should consider how to segment its customer base in such a way as to differentiate how customers use the library and how their expectations of service delivery might be different. Public libraries, more than likely, might want to segment responses by the thirteen "service responses" proposed in *Planning for Results.*[7]

It is also important to recognize that a library's customers most likely are not limited to in-house users and a geographically recognized boundary. Customers of world-class research universities, for instance, might be any scholar worldwide within a particular area of scholarship.[8] Thus, any survey would have to be adaptable to the Web and the delivery of electronic services to remote customers.

Staff Are Key

Professional and paraprofessional staff, as well as student workers, are on the front line, facing customers at every turn in the delivery of services. Their role in delivering satisfaction cannot be overstated. Nonetheless, the leadership role of the director and the rest of the management team should not be overlooked. The director is typically the driving force behind motivating and empowering employees to deliver satisfaction; "as a leader, showing your commitment to customer satisfaction will be essential to your [the library's] success. . . . Think like a customer, act like a leader."[9]

Interestingly, research shows that customer satisfaction and employee satisfaction are related. For instance, according to James L. Heskett, W. Earl Sasser Jr., and Leonard A. Schlesinger,

> [The correlation between customer satisfaction and employee satisfaction] has been found at every multiunit service organization for which we have data. . . . In all cases where data allow statistical analysis, the relationships are statistically significant. Other cases where data analysis was less precise nevertheless support the same conclusion. These and other experiences have led us to conclude that, in the absence of data regarding either customer or employee satisfaction, one can be predicted from the other. Show us an operating unit with higher employee satisfaction than another and we can predict with a high degree of reliability that its customers will also be more satisfied.[10]

The attitude and role of staff members are key to any service organization that values its customers. While the library has no choice over who its customers are, the library does control the selection of employees. For this reason, it makes sense to hire staff who have a customer service interest, indeed fervor; to train them accordingly; and to equip them with the authority to satisfy the customer within the context of the vision and mission of the library. This process begins by hiring the type of employee who is comfortable dealing with customers. The job candidate should understand how service quality and customer satisfaction relate to the library's mission. All the staff should be internally motivated to achieve this mission. Candidates can be told that meeting customer expectations is their job and that staff are expected to satisfy the customer within the mission of the library. The good hires will thrive on this responsibility and will take pride in their performance. Their enthusiasm will not go unnoticed by library customers. To the extent that existing staff may not already be internally motivated to provide customer satisfaction, an orientation program may help to so inspire them, or a reorganization involving shifts of responsibility may be in order. Failing all of these solutions, the library would be ill-advised to place staff who do not share a customer focus in direct contact with the public.

In any case, it makes sense to measure employee satisfaction from time to time. This is not difficult to do, but it requires a careful preliminary assessment of the internal political and management implications of doing so, as such a survey should signal that the organization is prepared to act and to change on the basis of what is learned. The focus is on organizational, not individual, performance.

There are many ways to measure employee satisfaction, such as with interviews, self-rating forms, focus groups, and formal surveys. One specific way to measure employee satisfaction is to use an employee satisfaction questionnaire. The value of such a questionnaire is that it gives employees a way to report how satisfied they are in their jobs and to offer suggestions for what could be done to improve the situation for them. Such a questionnaire can also ask them for their ideas on how to improve customer satisfaction.

Similarities between a customer satisfaction questionnaire and an employee satisfaction questionnaire are well founded. Both seek to assess perceived satisfaction, and both request an indication of how experience relates to expectations. Indeed, employees possess the same "expectations kernel" (see figure 3.1) as customers, though in connection with their job environment, their working experience, and their ability to carry out their jobs.

To further clarify the critical role of the employee in delivering satisfaction, figure 3.4 illustrates the employee-satisfaction nexus. There are two sides to this figure: the left side, which illustrates the relationship between the customer and the employee, and the right side, which shows the relationship between the employee and the employer. Beginning with the left side, the staff member is involved in delivering service to the customer, which results in a measurable degree of satisfaction for the customer, and, to the extent that the employee is motivated to serve the customer, also results in a measurable degree of satisfaction for the staff member.

The right side illustrates the relationship between the employee and the employer. The dynamics here involve the employee's performing within a job environment (including its ancillary attributes, such as compensation, benefits, and acknowledgment for doing well), which provides satisfaction to each staff member and, to the extent that the employee is satisfying the customer according to the mission of the library, satisfies the employer as well. This linkage of generating satisfaction, from the customer through to the employer, necessarily flows through and, in large measure, depends on the attitude, motivation, skill, and knowledge of the employee.

FIGURE 3.4
The Employee-Satisfaction Nexus

Following recruitment, each employee may be surveyed once every year or two. Depending on the organizational structure of the library, it may be appropriate to have division supervisors administer the questionnaire to their personnel. There is, however, good reason not to link this survey with any job performance review, as doing so may result in the employee's providing responses that he or she thinks may reflect favorably on performance. It is also important to attempt to shift the focus away from an individual and more toward a service.

Summary

Customer experiences with service delivery are changing more than ever. Not only are competitive enterprises continuously raising the bar to deliver outstanding service but new technology is opening up unprecedented ways to interact with customers. Customers are concomitantly raising their expectations of the quality of service delivery, and service providers that cannot keep pace with such expectations fall behind at their peril. While specific expectations are constantly changing, the underlying principles of how expectations are formed appear to be stable and provide a model for how libraries can influence expectations as a means to satisfy customers. This chapter reviewed several basic considerations important to understanding satisfaction and how it can be created and measured. The shift from a transaction relationship to a satisfaction relationship is essential, as is segmentation of the customer base. Undertaking a staff satisfaction survey, in addition to the customer satisfaction survey, is advantageous, since staff are key to delivering satisfaction to customers.

Customer satisfaction is not a passing fad.[11]

NOTES

1. William H. Davidow and Bro Uttal, *Total Customer Service: The Ultimate Weapon* (New York: Harper Perennial, 1989), 19.

2. David B. Pillemer, *Momentous Events, Vivid Memories: How Unforgettable Moments Help Us Understand the Meaning of Our Lives* (Cambridge, Mass.: Harvard University Press, 1998), 96.

3. John R. Whitman, *The Beneserve Customer Satisfaction System* (Wellesley, Mass.: Surveytools Corp., 1998).

4. Ibid.

5. See Allan B. Cox and Fred Gifford, "An Overview to Geographic Information Systems," *Journal of Academic Librarianship* 23, no. 6 (Nov. 1997): 449–61.

6. See Sandra Nelson, Ellen Altman, and Diane Mayo, *Managing for Results: Effective Resource Allocation for Public Libraries* (Chicago: American Library Assn., 2000), 36–8.

7. Ethel Himmel and William James Wilson, *Planning for Results: A Public Library Transformation Process*, 2 volumes (Chicago: American Library Assn., 1998).

8. See Rush G. Miller and Peter X. Zhou, "Global Resource Sharing: A Gateway Model," *Journal of Academic Librarianship* 25, no. 4 (July 1999): 281–7.

9. Whitman, *The Beneserve Customer Satisfaction System*, 7.

10. James L. Heskett, W. Earl Sasser Jr., and Leonard A. Schlesinger, *The Service Profit Chain: How Leading Companies Link Profit and Growth to Loyalty, Satisfaction, and Value* (New York: Free Press, 1997), 100–1.

11. Michael D. Johnson, *Customer Orientation and Market Action* (Upper Saddle River, N.J.: Prentice-Hall, 1998), 70.

4

The Framework for Improving Service Quality and Customer Satisfaction over Time

Libraries must become more customer-service oriented than ever before, with increased demand for services that are customized to meet the needs of particular clientele.[1]

A world-class organization's culture reflects its customers' beliefs.[2]

Libraries frequently have developed neither vision nor mission statements; furthermore, in those instances in which they have, these documents tend to focus on collections and constituencies served, rather than on services and customers. They also tend to be ignored once written. Moreover, libraries may not have established goals and objectives to set and meet service priorities and to ensure the accomplishment of the organizational mission. Thus, they tend to lack service priorities for the organization and a context for judging the extent to which they have been successful—that is, have met goals and semiannual or annual benchmarks. The purpose of this chapter is to set the stage for chapter 5 by reviewing vision and mission statements, standards, customer service plans, and measures (e.g., input, output, outcome, and customer) as elements of a library's strategic plan (see figure 4.1). The chapter offers the aforementioned guidance for libraries to set service priorities within the planning context and to measure their progress as they challenge themselves to improve the quality of service provided and to exceed (not merely meet) customer expectations. The desire is to achieve results-driven performance that puts customers first.

FIGURE 4.1
The Planning Process

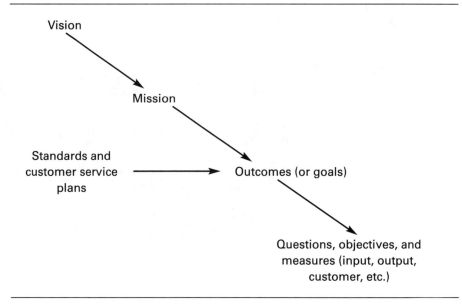

Planning

Planning involves a determination of appropriate goals for the library as a whole; a description of the current activities of the library and the effectiveness of those activities; an assessment of customer expectations and information needs and preferences; a determination of those services the library should provide; and formative (ongoing) and summative (at the end of a program) evaluation. Clearly, planning provides a direction and framework for library services and guides decision making. Strategic planning, "a self-analysis or self-study that identifies the organization's strengths and weaknesses and develops priorities within the framework of the organization's physical and financial capabilities," enables a library to decide which expectations it can and should treat as priorities.[3] As a consequence, planning directs and shapes the behavior exhibited by an organization.[4]

As part of the planning process, libraries can set customer service plans and pledges that represent organizational and service goals and develop annual objectives or targets to accomplish their aspirations. Is the library satisfied with its current level of service provision and the receptivity of its customers to that level, or does it seek improvement? As well, how much of the community might be counted as customers—satisfied and delighted ones?

Vision Statements

As Jann E. Freed and Marie R. Klugman write,

A vision statement is a philosophy about values; it is futuristic and optimistic. In contrast, a mission statement is more specifically focused; it outlines the institution's purpose and differentiates the institution from other institutions. A vision statement answers the question: Where do we want to be in five to ten years, and what do we want to be doing? On the other hand, a mission statement answers the question: What is our purpose?[5]

A vision statement must nonetheless display a sense of reality: The library must be able to "develop the capacity to address [the promise] during the course of the planning cycle."[6] That statement shapes the direction depicted by the mission statement.

Mission Statements

Many organizations have developed mission statements, but such statements should not be written and then discarded. They are a linchpin of the planning process.

Academe

According to Robert C. Dickeson, a mission statement is "the academic grid against which all evaluation of programs [and services] must be measured. . . . A limitless mission is of minimal use in a time of imposing limits."

> Speaking in lofty terms about the discovery and transmission of knowledge, the value of wisdom, and the regard for the individual, mission statements typically lack sufficient clarity to articulate to audiences, internal and external, specific understanding about the institution, its purposes, or its future.
>
> Mission statements are typically written in language vague and timeless enough to appeal to the ages, to cover all eventualities, and to serve in as overarching a stretch as possible. This limitless dimension is designed to cover whatever new notion or program may emerge in the future, and in a time of rapid change, a generalized mission affords protection against the unforeseeable.[7]

Turning to what a mission statement should contain, Dickeson says it "address[es] unique roles and scope of the institution" and "the specific ways . . . [the institution fulfills its] most essential purposes." For community colleges, Dickeson states, there are typically five purposes:

1. *The transfer mission:* preparing students to transfer to four-year colleges and universities
2. *The career preparation mission:* preparing students for new careers, career changes, and career advancement
3. *The developmental education mission:* expanding higher education opportunities to populations previously unserved
4. *The continuing education and community service mission:* serving the expressed economic development needs of college constituents and communities
5. *The access mission:* providing for universal access to higher education[8]

Four-year academic institutions with a liberal arts tradition also espouse five purposes:

1. Preparing students for careers
2. Transmitting the civilization
3. Teaching how to think
4. Liberating the individual ("Graduates should view who they are and how they fit into this world in changed ways")
5. Teaching values

For research universities, the imperative is to add to as well as draw from the fund of knowledge. This mission is buttressed by significant increases in external support for research dollars, new partnerships with business and industry to help solve some of society's most pressing problems, and new calls for involving students in hands-on research at ever earlier stages in their education.[9]

In his assessment, Dickeson calls for the reexamination of mission statements and their accommodation for a "new emphasis on learning" (serving as a "learning community"), reflection of the "benefits of higher education," and "focusing on competencies." The benefits might be

public economic (e.g., increased tax revenues, greater productivity, and increased workforce flexibility)

private economic (e.g., higher salaries and benefits, employment, improved working conditions, and personal and professional mobility)

public social (e.g., increased charitable giving and community service, increased quality of civic life, and improved ability to adapt to and use technology)

private social (e.g., improved health and life expectancy, improved quality of life for offspring, and increased personal status)[10]

As employers place increased demands on institutions of higher education to "deliver graduates more readily able to work," the demand for competency-based learning will continue to grow and to emphasize "base competencies (such as mobilizing innovation and change, managing people and tasks, communicating, and managing self); general knowledge and values to understand the world; specific skills in an area of expertise; and specific knowledge in an area of 'knowledge that is transient.'"[11]

In summary,

[The] mission should permit only those activities that need to be done and that the institution and its people do well. The mission, a synthesis of the college's functions, purposes, and values, should summon the institution to its future, not its past. It should resolve conflicts over what the college does, why it exists, and whom it serves. It should take into account the likely forces that will affect its students' lives in the future.[12]

The mission should be coupled with a vision statement and a strategic plan, one that focuses on strategic directions and people, not things, and that guides the determination and realization of institutional priorities. Both the mission and vision statements are key aspects of continuous improvement. Such improvement ensures that goals match and achieve the institution's mission. As a result, it is essential that all members of the institution or organization be informed of the vision and mission statements and that these statements guide their day-to-day work.

The library's mission naturally should be in line with that of the institution and guide the managerial decisions made. The planning process should also be linked to the institutional mission and vision.

Public Libraries

The American Library Association's *Planning for Results* encourages public libraries to conduct a "community scan" and a "library scan," and, from these activities, to develop a mission statement that summarizes the service responses the library has selected.[13] There are at least thirteen service responses that describe most of the services offered by public libraries:

Basic literacy . . . addresses the need to read and perform other essential daily tasks

Business and career information . . . addresses a need for information related to business, careers, work, entrepreneurship, personal finances, and obtaining employment

Commons . . . helps address the need of people to meet and interact with others in their community and to participate in public discourse about community issues

Community referral . . . addresses the need for information related to services provided by community agencies and organizations

Consumer information . . . addresses the need for information to make informed consumer decisions and to help community residents become more self-sufficient

Cultural awareness . . . helps satisfy the desire of community residents to gain an understanding of their own cultural heritage and the cultural heritage of others

Current topics and titles . . . helps to fulfill community residents' appetite for information about popular cultural and social trends and their desire for satisfying recreational experiences

Formal learning support . . . helps students who are enrolled in a formal program of education or who are pursuing their education through a program of home-schooling to attain their educational goals

General information . . . helps meet the need for information and answers to questions on a broad array of topics related to work, school, and personal life

Government information . . . helps satisfy the need for information about elected officials and government agencies that enables people to participate in the democratic process

Information literacy . . . helps address the need for skills related to finding, evaluating, and using information effectively

Lifelong learning . . . helps address the desire for self-directed personal growth and development opportunities

Local history and genealogy . . . addresses the desire of community residents to know and better understand personal or community heritage.[14]

Since many public libraries function in a political environment, one dependent on taxpayer support, they dare not limit the service responses to a few choices. Rather, they must attempt to support all thirteen service responses to some degree. Since trying to provide "something for everyone" depletes scarce resources, libraries need service priorities.

Planning for Results offers excellent advice on the practical nature of mission statements.

> Make sure that you're prepared to deliver on what you promise in your mission statement. You will be using this mission statement to inform community members about what you do and to encourage them to use your services. If you can't deliver what you promise, your mission statement will do more harm than good.[15]

Standards

Association standards set acceptable levels of performance for any institution seeking accreditation. The purpose of these standards is to define minimum levels of expectations that institutions must strive to meet or that they do not fall below. Standards view an institution as part of a larger grouping—all institutions under the jurisdiction of the association—and offer a base of general comparison.

The draft of standards for college libraries contains a section on services.

> The library should establish, promote, and maintain a range and quality of services that will support the college's mission and goals. The library should provide competent and prompt assistance for its users. Hours of access to the library should be reasonable and convenient for its users. Reference and other special assistance should be available at times when the college's primary users most need it. When academic programs are offered at off-campus sites, library services should be provided in accordance with ACRL's [Association of College and Research Libraries] "Guidelines for Extended Campus Library Services."[16]

The evaluation section of the standards draft raises eight questions for librarians and academic administrators to consider as they address effectiveness.

1. How well does the library establish, promote, and maintain a range and quality of services that support the academic program of the college and encourage optimal library use?

2. How are reference services designed to teach users ways to take full advantage of the resources available to them?

3. How do the expectations of the students and faculty affect library services?

4. Are loan policies equitable and uniformly administered to all qualified users?

5. Does the library maintain hours of access consistent with reasonable demand?

6. What library services are provided for programs at off-campus sites? How are the needs of users and their satisfaction determined at those sites?

7. How are students and faculty informed of library services?

8. Does the library maintain and utilize quantitative and qualitative measurements of its ability to service its clientele?[17]

Service Plans

As Amos Lakos explains, "it is essential that the value of quality, in particular the focus on delivering service quality be the core value of the library. . . . Understanding and digestion of this value into every decision and every process," he maintains, "should be the basic tenet of the library."[18] National governments, including those of the United States and Great Britain, as well as some academic and public libraries have introduced quality service plans and pledges and have developed ways to track the extent to which the entire organization is committed to providing outstanding customer service and to meeting the plans and pledges.[19]

As Susan Wehmeyer, Dorothy Auchter, and Arnold Hirshon explain, a service pledge is part of an overall service plan.

> The plan includes the entire spectrum of customer service improvement efforts, such as the means to derive customer input and satisfaction (surveys, focus groups, etc.), staff customer-service training programs, and organizational response mechanisms. The customer service pledge is a published statement, prepared after consultation with all staff, that articulates the intentions of the organization to provide meaningful and measurable levels of quality service. The pledge may contain both broad services, as well as specific and objective criteria by which to judge how adequately the organization is meeting these goals.[20]

The pledge, a brief document written from the customer's point of view, may be (but does not have to be) shared with customers and it "serves as a public commitment to provide specific [ongoing] services at or above a minimal standard."[21] It might be that the library wants to treat the pledge as an internal document that challenges the staff to improve the quality of services provided.

At no point should staff be individually evaluated against the promises contained in the pledge as part of their annual performance. Such a misuse of the pledge places pressure on the individual, rather than on the service as a whole, and may make staff resist change.

Naturally, creation and implementation of a service plan and pledge require the full support of the library director and the rest of the senior management team. The pledge lets the staff determine service priorities and underscores the service commitment of the organization. To meet the service promises, the director may have to either expend additional resources or reallocate existing resources (e.g., reassign staff or restructure the organization).

Promises in the pledge are grouped by service areas, not department, and are specific, objective, and positively phrased. There is no qualification such as "usually" or "generally." Furthermore, any promises must be clear to the customers.

Presumably, approximately every five years as organizations continue to change, libraries should revisit and replace their pledge with one that reflects new service commitments and promises. The purpose is to change the organization on a continual basis.

Goals and Objectives

The literature of library and information science has often stated that "the effectiveness of the organization and its various activities cannot be determined without a statement of goals and objectives, because, by definition, effectiveness is the degree to which the library accomplishes objectives."[22] *Goals* are long-term aspirations that the organization intends to meet, while *objectives* are clear and balanced guides to action, explicit enough to suggest certain types of actions, time-limited, feasible, and measurable. Objectives lead to the realization of a goal and should be "ambitious enough to be challenging."[23]

Goals, and objectives as well, might relate to services, resource management, or administration. Both goals and objectives reflect priorities—"what is most important (not unimportant)."[24] Sources such as *Planning for Results* offer examples of both goals and objectives.[25] The next section offers alternatives to goals—outcomes—and to objectives—measures.

Evaluation Questions and Measures

Staff set evaluation questions and measures within the context of the library's mission statements. These questions and measures guide data collection and, if addressed on a recurring basis, indicate the progress that the library makes in meeting its goals.

Performance Measurement and Performance-Based Management

As discussed in *Assessing Service Quality*, librarians have choices about where they concentrate their evaluation efforts to achieve performance-based management. Information managers might use performance measurement data to help set agreed-upon performance goals for the organization and staff, to allocate and prioritize resources, to either confirm or change current policy or program directions to meet those goals, and to report on the success in meeting those goals. They might examine one or more of the following questions:

How much?	How well?
How many?	How valuable?
How economical?	How reliable?
How prompt?	How courteous?
How accurate?	How satisfied?[26]
How responsive?	

These questions can be recast as *output, outcome,* and *customer-related* measures that are part of a clear and cohesive performance measurement framework, one that is understood by all levels of the organization and that links measures to goals and the ongoing collection of data. Alternatively, the questions could be framed as objectives. A library will, therefore, have to decide whether to use questions, objectives, or measures. Whatever the decision, the questions, objectives, or measures selected should be meaningful to the organization and its customers and show "How are we doing?" or "Are we progressing to reach some end?"

Performance measurement involves comparison with goals and target levels of intended accomplishment. In contrast, performance-based management essentially uses performance information either to manage better, to improve program effectiveness, or to interact with people who control resources to demonstrate what the program or service accomplished so they commit the resources to keep what they deemed to be priority programs operational.

Types of Measures for Academic Libraries

The previously mentioned draft of the standards for college libraries explains that "earlier standards . . . relied heavily upon resource and program 'inputs' such as money, space, materials, and staff activities. These new standards continue to consider 'inputs,' but they also take into consideration 'outputs' and 'outcomes.'" The standards offer the following definitions:

> Inputs are generally regarded as the raw materials of a library program—the money, space, collection, equipment, and staff out of which a program can arise

> Outputs serve to quantify the work done, i.e., number of books circulated, number of reference questions answered
>
> Outcomes are the ways in which library users are changed as a result of their contact with the libraries' resources and programs[27]

An example of an input measure is the percentage of the total library budget expended for materials or information resources, staff, and all other operating expenses. An output measure might be the ratio of reference questions (for a sample week) to combined student and faculty full-time equivalents; or correct answer fill rate, the percentage of questions correctly answered.[28]

Inputs comprise the resources available, but they might also be viewed as resources consumed. At the same time, performance measurement has been defined differently, but it often embraces inputs, outputs, and processes. Clearly, the nomenclature cannot be rigidly applied and has been known to vary among organizations. Karen V. Bottrill and Victor M. H. Borden provided an extensive list of measures that serve as performance indicators for higher education; some evaluators would label process measures as either inputs or outputs.[29] Nonetheless, figure 4.2 reprints those indicators that are most relevant to academic libraries. Those indicators, as well as the efforts to develop a library performance measurement and quality management system that produces a set of performance indicators for an electronic environment (PIEE), in a number of instances fail to reflect the perspectives, expectations, and satisfaction of library users, as well as service-related outcomes. Examples of PIEE are

> percentage of target population reached by electronic library services
>
> number of log-ons to electronic library services per capita per month
>
> number of remote log-ons to electronic library services per capita per month
>
> number of electronic documents delivered per capita per month
>
> cost per log-on per electronic library service
>
> reference inquiries submitted electronically per capita per month
>
> number of library computer workstations per capita
>
> mean waiting time for access to library computer workstations
>
> information technology expenditure as a percentage of total library expenditure[30]

Arguably, except for "mean waiting time," these measures are inputs or outputs. Mean waiting time may produce a number unacceptable to the library's customers. In fact, regardless of the mean waiting time, the absolute number of customers kept waiting for a lengthy period may be unacceptable. Of course, the library must define the population using its electronic services in order to calculate a meaningful percentage.

Although figure 4.2 and this section are slanted toward academic libraries, public libraries can adapt the discussion to fit their circumstances.

FIGURE 4.2

Examples of Performance Indicators

General Areas	Indicator	Input	Process	Output
Collaboration	Percentage of students reporting having visited faculty during office hours	x		
	Percentage of faculty reporting involvement with a student club or organization	x		
Community needs	Number of outside groups using college facilities		x	
	Cultural activities for outside groups: number, duration, and participation		x	
Completers	Satisfaction levels of graduates			x
Curriculum	Percentage of courses requiring students to engage in independent research papers, projects, presentations, or similar exercises [requiring use of the library]		x	
	Student satisfaction with instruction, programs, and services		x	
	Degree of innovation or degree of innovative orientation		x	
	Total number of enrollments by course	x		
	Enrollment per section	x		
Facilities	Use of facilities by departments		x	
	Amount of software per student in the audiovisual center [or elsewhere]	x		
	Number of volumes or books per student in the library	x		
	Telecommunications and computing resources	x		
	Resources for scholarly and creative activity	x		
	Resources for research activity and quality of research output	x		
Faculty	Teaching awards and recognition		x	
	Percentage of full-time faculty who are tenured	x		
	Number of faculty research or development grants awarded annually			x
	Books produced by staff each year			x
	Chapters produced by staff in books per year			x

(continued)

FIGURE 4.2

Examples of Performance Indicators (continued)

General Areas	Indicator	Input	Process	Output
Faculty (continued)	Journal publications produced by staff per year by type of journal (refereed, peer reviewed)			x
	National, regional, and local papers presented			x
	Average number of conferences organized, attended			x
	Percentage of time spent on research		x	
	Contributions to professional organizations			x
	Consultancies to community organizations			x
	Participation in editorial staff of books and journals			x
Finances	Library support compared with that at peer institutions	x		
	Percentage of costs for library, audiovisual centers		x	
	Percentage expenditure on innovation projects		x	
	Percentage of budget spent on continuing training		x	
	Library costs per student		x	
	Expenditure on computer services		x	
Special populations	Programs and services for reentry and nontraditional students	x		
Teaching/learning	Percentage of courses requiring students to use the library as a research resource		x	
	Number of items checked out of the library by undergraduates and so forth		x	
	Percentage of available library study spaces occupied by students		x	
	Percentage of students completing their first year without checking a book out of the library		x	

Adapted from Karen V. Bottrill and Victor M. H. Borden, "Appendix: Examples from the Literature," *New Directions for Institutional Research* 82 (summer 1994): 107–17.

The shift to electronic service delivery affects all libraries, but whatever measures they select should not be limited to inputs and outputs. As attention begins to focus on outcomes and the customers, new measures can be adapted to meet the needs of libraries and reflect the priorities of their customers.

The Association of College and Research Libraries (ACRL) Task Force on Academic Library Outcomes Assessment, like the standards for college libraries, defines outcomes as "the ways in which library users are changed as a result of their contact with the libraries' resources and programs." Surprisingly, the Task Force views satisfaction and dissatisfaction as "facile" outcomes that are

> too often unrelated to more substantial outcomes that hew more closely to the missions of libraries and the institutions they serve. The important outcomes of an academic library program involve the answers to questions like these:
>
>> Is the academic performance of students improved through their contact with the library?
>>
>> By using the library, do students improve their chances of having a successful career?
>>
>> Are undergraduates who used the library more likely to succeed in graduate school?
>>
>> Does the library's bibliographic instruction program result in a high level of "information literacy" among students?
>>
>> As a result of collaboration with the library's staff, are faculty members more likely to view use of the library as an integral part of their courses?
>>
>> Are students who use the library more likely to lead fuller and more satisfying lives?[31]

The Task Force correctly concludes that, for "accrediting agencies and state education authorities' accountability requirements . . . [rigorous measurement] is not necessary to produce meaningful results." Further, the Task Force recognizes that these questions are difficult to answer but encourages research to pursue such questions and craft the next generation of standards for academic libraries.[32]

The Task Force also maintains that "the purpose of all inputs—whether of the resource [such as a database subscription or a staff member] or program [such as a bibliographic instruction session or any interlibrary loan service] variety—is to achieve *outcomes*."[33] Evidently, for the Task Force, measuring program outcomes is the primary indicator of quality for higher education.

Limiting outcome measurement to change among users through their contact with the library's resources and programs short-changes the opportunity the library has to reach out to potential customers. As presented in chapter 1, customers comprise four groups, only one of which can be classified as actual users—present customers. The other groups, which together comprise noncustomers, are

> never-gained customers (have not yet experienced the services of a particular library—e.g., incoming college freshmen or new members of a community)
>
> lost customers (dissatisfied with the service provided and unwilling to revisit)
>
> noncustomers (unwilling to visit under any circumstances)

An important question is "Might library services have an impact on these other groups and convert them to customers?" Moreover, many library customers prefer to be self-sufficient or self-reliant, and the users of library Web sites could be anywhere—local, regional, statewide, national, or international. Thus, in an electronic information age, the population served might not be known: it might be anyone with access to the Internet. Furthermore, an outcome such as the "student matches [his or her] information needs to information resources and can organize an effective search strategy" is something that is more important to the library than to customers, especially when students, for instance, have choices among the information providers (e.g., bookstores, the Internet, and libraries) they choose to consult.[34]

Finally, questions such as "Are students who use the library more likely to lead fuller and more satisfying lives?" will not readily produce quantitative data—a ratio and a percentage (see chapter 8)—primarily due to the vague terms used. It is also impossible to answer such questions without using complex experimental designs in which researchers manipulate variables, control for masking (variables operating in the background and exerting an influence over other variables), apply parametric statistics, and carefully define terms (e.g., "use" and "fuller and more satisfying lives").

It is most likely that outcomes have two contexts, namely:

1. learning objectives that the library expects to attain (e.g., "Have the students who attended a bibliographic instruction program acquired the knowledge and developed the skills that are identified as the program's objectives?") or the results that a program, service, or activity is expected to achieve (e.g., "Is your program educating its students appropriately? Are they learning what the program teaches?")[35]

2. goals that a library wants to attain (e.g., "By the year 2004, 80 percent of library users will successfully access resources available through the library's World Wide Web site without staff intervention"), and the measurement of incremental progress toward the accomplishment of that target

The first type of outcome measures might involve an assessment of the results of a program activity or service as compared with its intended purpose. Such measures examine what the organization wants to achieve but do not necessarily address customer expectations. Only the second type of measures has a customer focus. At any rate, for outcome measurement to occur, library staff must define the service or program target that they expect to achieve. The library, of course, must be willing to commit the necessary resources to meet the priorities established.

Customer-focused outcomes related to satisfaction and the achievement of a customer service plan can be easily formulated, and the extent of their accomplishment directly measured. Such outcomes are indeed "facile"; they reflect a service orientation and place the meeting of customer expectations first. On the other hand, it may be exceedingly difficult to assess the attainment of a student learning outcome such as

All graduates are information literate, prepared to be lifelong learners able to effectively identify, access, and use a variety of information resources; proficient with appropriate information technologies; and able to evaluate and apply information to meet academic, personal, and job-related needs.[36]

Inadequate insights into the extent to which the outcome is realized are gained by, for instance, counting the number of student participants; having self-rating forms for freshmen and sophomores to complete; and gathering student, faculty, and employer perceptions about whether the outcome was met. Clearly, the outcome has some complex elements that are difficult to measure with any validity (e.g., "all," "lifelong learners," "able to effectively . . . ," "proficient," and "able to evaluate and apply").[37]

ACRL has developed *Information Literacy Competency Standards for Higher Education* that identifies standards, performance indicators, and measurable outcomes.[38] The proposed outcomes ought to be viewed as taking the incoming freshman class and ensuring that they have gained certain knowledge and skills upon graduation. In such a case, academic libraries would have to set semester and annual targets as well as gain the support of faculty in subject departments about these targets, outcomes, performance indicators, and standards. A further complication is that some of the outcomes (e.g., "participates in class discussions . . . ") are subjective and do not deal with the quality and relevance of that discussion. Furthermore, other outcomes require the use of multiple methods of assessment, some of which are quite complex. Many libraries lack the resources, including time, to verify the achievement of multiple outcomes. Clearly, thinking about widely acceptable outcome assessment is at a preliminary stage.

To the list of types of measures (input, output, and outcome measures), there should be added mention of impact measures, "the direct or indirect effects or consequences resulting from achieving program goals."[39] According to one source,

> Measuring program impact often is done by comparing program outcomes with estimates of the outcomes that would have occurred in the absence of the program. . . . One example of measuring direct impact is to compare the outcome for a randomly assigned group receiving a service with the outcome for a randomly assigned group not receiving the service.[40]

An alternate (and dubiously demonstrative) definition of impact is "how a service made a difference in some other activity or situation, for example, freshmen who took a library Internet training program had, on average, a letter grade higher in their English class than those freshmen who did not take the class."[41] Impacts might also be economic in nature and deal with arbitrary terminology such as "expected" and "significant" impacts.[42] Clearly, libraries might like to pursue impact assessment, but, given the complex research designs needed, will rarely do so.

Customer Perspective

Five of the previously mentioned eleven evaluation questions reflect the following customer perspectives:

How well? How responsive?

How valuable? How satisfied?

How reliable?

When evaluators want the perspective of the library, of the broader organization of which the library is a part, or of society, then the other six questions previously mentioned become relevant.[43] Whichever question is selected, it could be converted into a measure and examined in terms of a goal and ongoing progress toward its attainment. Thus, it is possible that the question or measure could easily serve as a replacement for the setting of objectives.

The Planning Process: Examples

The previous section discussed the various parts of the planning process: vision and mission statements, goals and objectives, customer service pledge, input and output measures, and outcome and customer measures. The purpose of this section is to identify specific examples of each so that librarians can review their own documentation and ensure that customers receive proper notice in key documentation and in the planning process.

Vision Statements

Apparently, few libraries place either their mission or vision statements on their World Wide Web home pages. The Indiana University library at Bloomington, however, provides both. The mission emphasizes a commitment.

> To support and strengthen teaching, learning, and research by providing the collections, services, and environments that lead to intellectual discovery.

The vision states that

> We will provide the University with state-of-the-art library resources and associated services by
>
> • Providing innovative service to our clientele, who will become increasingly diverse, non-traditional, interdisciplinary, and located at remote sites;
> • Exercising vigorous management of our rich and varied collections;
> • Making our collections known to others through teaching and publication;
> • Making connections to national and global resources that support scholarship and creativity;
> • Cultivating a physical and electronic environment that promotes teaching, learning, and scholarship;
> • Exerting leadership in information technology within the University and at state and national levels to support student learning, educational attainment, and research; and

- Achieving excellence, efficiency, diversity, and accountability in our staff at all levels.[44]

Wright State University Libraries, in Dayton, Ohio, has a "Diversity Vision Statement."

> The University Libraries are committed to promoting an educational, cultural, and work environment that is responsive to Wright State University's increasingly multicultural community. Accordingly the Libraries will foster and encourage sensitivity to diversity among its patrons and staff and will continuously work to further the intellectual diversity of its collections and services.
>
> In its important role of supporting the teaching, research, and service missions of the University, the Libraries collect and facilitate access to information and ideas. We affirm that knowledge will advance and intellectual excellence flourish as a direct result of diverse experiences and viewpoints shared freely in an open environment.
>
> We are strongly committed to providing our community with equitable access to the Libraries' resources, and to our employees, equal advancement opportunities without regard to race, sex, creed, color, religion, national origin, sexual orientation, ancestry, age, marital status, handicap, or veteran status. We . . . [are] also strongly committed to provide our staff with a workplace free from prejudice and discrimination, where the personal dignity and worth of each individual is appreciated and celebrated.
>
> We invite members of the University community to suggest ways that we may advance this policy.[45]

Mission Statements

Academic Institutions

For the profiles, including the mission statements, of ten academic institutions—ranging from community colleges to research universities—see Freed and Klugman.[46] The home pages of many institutions also report mission statements.

Academic Libraries

Mission Statements for College Libraries reprints 52 examples, categorized according to control (public and private) and number of students (more or less than 2,500).[47] In addition, the mission statement of the University of Maryland Libraries is

> The Libraries' Mission is to contribute to the University's academic excellence by
>
> - Identifying recorded knowledge and developing organized collections relevant to the University's mission and creating intellectual tools to utilize these collections;
> - Contributing to the advancement of information access, storage, retrieval, use, and preservation;

- Ensuring easy access to and use of information and knowledge, regardless of medium;
- Instructing patrons in critical skills related to research;
- Promoting information literacy and lifelong learning;
- Assisting patrons in their use of information resources;
- Preserving the cultural and intellectual heritage of humankind; and
- Providing an intellectual center for the University.

In contributing to the University's academic excellence, the Libraries strive

- To achieve the highest standards of quality in the intellectual resources and services provided;
- To draw upon the minds of those with the best talents and insights for building the Libraries' services and resources to support campus instruction and research;
- To adapt library resources, services, and management in an era of constant change;
- To foster services to diverse populations and promote diversity among the staff; and
- To ensure freedom of access to information to all users.[48]

The mission of the Massachusetts Institute of Technology (MIT) Libraries is

> The MIT Libraries are creative partners in the research and learning process. We select, organize, present, and preserve information resources relevant to education and research at MIT. We sustain these world-class resources and provide quality services on behalf of the present and future research and scholarly community. We build intellectual connections among these resources and educate the MIT community in the effective use of information. We want to be the place people in the MIT community think of first when they need information.[49]

Sawyer Library, Suffolk University, has as its mission to contribute

> to the overall mission of the University by making available, and providing access to, informational resources and qualified staff to support the teaching, learning, and research needs of . . . students, faculty, and staff. It participates in the University's effort to teach students the skills they need to find and evaluate information, to learn rather than amass information, and to turn information into knowledge. The Sawyer Library also provides a place for students and faculty to read and study, to gather and deliberate, and to question, challenge, and support one another. It is a goal that all members of the University community become independent, self-sufficient, self-directed, lifelong information users.[50]

Following the mission statement are goals (for information resources, information services, and support structures) and objectives. Appendix A at the end of this chapter presents the goals and selected objectives of Sawyer Library, Suffolk University. These objectives have been converted into measurable statements. (See http://www.suffolk.edu/admin/sawlib/plans/htm.)

ACRL has developed a model mission statement for university undergraduate libraries.[51] For a community college, "the . . . statement serves as a 'unique window through which . . . [the learning resources center gains] a clearer understanding' of the learning resources center's role in the college."[52] The mission of one health sciences library follows.

[The University of North Carolina at Chapel Hill Health Sciences Library's mission] is to manage information and knowledge to advance health, by providing access to information and knowledge and educating users to manage information and knowledge; by creating and maintaining accurate, reliable, integrated information and knowledge systems; by participating actively in the development of information and knowledge management policies; and by conducting and promoting research in information and library science.[53]

Public Libraries

For examples of mission statements for public libraries, see Robert D. Stueart and Barbara B. Moran.[54] A proposed model mission statement for public libraries mentions that

The mission of the _____ Library is to provide informational, cultural, educational and recreational resources and services to the people of _____ city, as well as the metro area and the state. The Library seeks to accomplish its mission through prudent management and development of its resources and by providing access to a broad range of materials and services to meet the present and the future needs of the community it serves. The Library will cooperate with other libraries, educational, cultural, community, and government agencies and institutions and the Library supports freedom of information for all.[55]

That mission statement, as well as those statements given in appendix B at the end of this chapter, might require some reworking to address service responses.

Customer Service Pledge

Appendix C, at the end of this chapter, reproduces Wright State University Libraries' revised pledge, "Commitment to Excellence." (The result is a shorter document than that which appeared in *Service Quality for Academic Libraries*.) The pledge identifies the services offered; some of the items pledged are quantifiable and others are not. For instance, the library can easily monitor whether current periodicals are shelved "within twenty-four hours of receipt," whereas "initiate searches for missing materials" does not specify any time frame.

Any library could review such a pledge to see what services will be offered, what the staff are willing to identify as priority activities, and where the management team is willing to commit scarce resources.

Libraries might extend their pledge to include their Web site. For example,

- The information content is up-to-date.

- It takes no more than three clicks of the mouse to find what you need.
- Graphical images are easy to follow and expedite the location of information.

If there is a digital library collection, it might also be covered by the pledge. Libraries might also have a section of the home page devoted to frequently asked questions that in part, respond to letters of complaint.

Input and Output Measures

Standards and guidelines frequently contain study questions and recommend input and output measures to pursue, but these measures tend not to focus on customer expectations and satisfaction.[56] *Planning for Results* also identifies output measures for the thirteen service responses but likewise does not make a connection to customers.[57]

Customer-Related Measures

Numerous examples of customer-related measures appear in *Service Quality for Academic Libraries* and *Assessing Service Quality*.[58] As they establish such measures, libraries might review chapter 2 and set benchmarks to improve service performance over time. For example, statement 4a of figure 2.1 asks respondents to rate staff as approachable and welcoming. Libraries can try to improve their performance on these attributes between surveys. They could also set a level of performance to achieve with each survey.

Summary

Institutional effectiveness examines the capacity of an institution to assess, verify, and enhance the fulfillment of its mission and purposes. Effectiveness may focus on the attainment of educational objectives, such as those relating to bibliographic instruction and information literacy. Academic and some public libraries are also "expected to document how their performance contributes to institutional goals and outcomes." To demonstrate accountability and as part of continuous quality improvement, they may engage in self-examination and seek to ascertain how well they achieve their service claims and to determine where improvement is needed. However, the assessment process links the mission statement to the setting of service priorities, the gathering of evidence, the interpretation of that evidence (in the context of outcomes and appropriate questions or measures), and a determination of the extent to which the priorities are attained. Clearly, the key is to link institutional effectiveness to planning, decision making, and the allocation and best use of scarce resources; and to meet the critical needs of the institution or organization. It is essential to accomplish these activities while never forgetting the importance of customers to the institution's or organization's mission and vision. After all, should not the library be a customer-driven organization?

In the broadest sense, the culture of an organization is interpreted by customers through both direct and indirect experience. The overall quality of service provided tends to be defined by customers based on their cumulative experiences with the organization.[59]

NOTES

1. Arnold Hirshon, "Libraries, Consortia, and Change Management," *Journal of Academic Librarianship* 25, no. 2 (March 1999): 124.

2. U.S. National Performance Review, *World-Class Courtesy: A Best Practices Report* (Washington, D.C.: GPO, 1997), section 1.1. Available: http://www.npr.gov/library/papers/benchmrk/courtesy/chapter1.html.

3. Thomas A. Childers and Nancy A. Van House, *What's Good? Describing Your Public Library's Effectiveness* (Chicago: American Library Assn., 1993), 18.

4. Robert D. Stueart and Barbara B. Moran, *Library and Information Center Management*, 5th ed. (Englewood, Colo.: Libraries Unlimited, 1998), 44.

5. Jann E. Freed and Marie R. Klugman, *Quality Principles and Practices in Higher Education: Different Questions for Different Times* (Phoenix, Ariz.: Oryx, 1997), 59.

6. Ethel Himmel and William James Wilson, with the ReVision Committee of the Public Library Association, *Planning for Results: A Public Library Transformation Process: The Guidebook* (Chicago: American Library Assn., 1998), 25.

7. Robert C. Dickeson, *Prioritizing Academic Programs and Services: Reallocating Resources to Achieve Strategic Balance* (San Francisco: Jossey-Bass, 1999), 29–30.

8. Ibid., both quotations, 31, 35–6.

9. Ibid., both quotations, 36–8.

10. Ibid., both quotations, 39–40.

11. Ibid., 40.

12. Ibid., 41.

13. Himmel and Wilson, *Planning for Results: The Guidebook*, 21, 23.

14. Ethel Himmel and William James Wilson, with the ReVision Committee of the Public Library Association, *Planning for Results: A Public Library Transformation Process: How-to-Do-It Manual* (Chicago: American Library Assn., 1998), m1–m2 (Workform M, "Service Response Summary").

15. Himmel and Wilson, *Planning for Results: The Guidebook*, 31.

16. "Standards for College Libraries: A Draft," *College & Research Libraries News* 60, no. 5 (May 1999): 377.

17. Ibid., 375, 377.

18. Amos Lakos, "Building a Culture of Assessment in Academic Libraries—Obstacles and Possibilities" (paper presented at Living the Future II, Tucson, Ariz., 22 April 1998), 6.

19. See U.S. National Performance Review, *Putting Customers First: Standards for Serving the American People* (Washington, D.C.: GPO, 1994), available: http://www.npr.gov; Jo Aitkins, "Setting Standards and Monitoring Performance: The Experience of Information Services at the University of Sunderland," in *Proceedings of the 2nd Northumbria International Conference on Performance Measurement in Libraries and Information Services* (Newcastle upon Tyne, Engl.: Information North, 1998), 101–4. For the "Wright State University Libraries' Pledge and Commitment to Excellence," see Peter Hernon and Ellen Altman, *Service Quality in Academic Libraries* (Norwood, N.J.: Ablex, 1996), 59–60. For the "Lehigh University Information Resources Service Standards," see Peter Hernon and Ellen Altman, *Assessing Service Quality: Satisfying the Expectations of Library Customers* (Chicago: American Library Assn., 1998), 39–41.

20. Susan Wehmeyer, Dorothy Auchter, and Arnold Hirshon, "Saying What We Will Do, and Doing What We Say: Implementing a Customer Service Plan," *Journal of Academic Librarianship* 22, no. 3 (May 1996): 173.

21. Ibid., 175.

22. Peter Hernon and Charles R. McClure, *Evaluation and Library Decision Making* (Norwood, N.J.: Ablex, 1990), 21.

23. See Charles H. Granger, "The Hierarchy of Objectives," *Harvard Business Review* 42, no. 3 (May–June, 1964): 64–5.

24. Hernon and McClure, *Evaluation and Library Decision Making*, 21.

25. Himmel and Wilson, *Planning for Results: The Guidebook*, 43–5. Also: *Planning for Results: A How-to-Do-It Manual*, 59–78.

26. See Hernon and Altman, *Assessing Service Quality*, 51–5.

27. "Standards for College Libraries," both quotations, 375.

28. See *Information and Documentation—Library Performance Indicators* (Geneva, Switz.: International Organization for Standardization, 1998).

29. Karen V. Bottrill and Victor M. H. Borden, "Appendix: Examples from the Literature," *New Directions for Institutional Research* 82 (summer 1994): 107.

30. EQUINOX: Library Performance Measurement and Quality Management System (funded under the Telematics for Libraries Programme of the European Commission), "Initial Definition of Electronic Performance Indicators." Available: http://equinox.dcu.ie/reports/pilist.html.

31. Assn. of College and Research Libraries, Task Force on Academic Library Outcomes Assessment, *Report* (June 27, 1998), 3. Available: http://www.ala.org/acrl/outcome.html.

32. Ibid.

33. Ibid., 4.

34. Quotation from Assn. of College and Research Libraries, *Report*, 6.

35. American Library Assn., Committee on Accreditation, *Outcomes Assessment for Library and Information Studies: Resource Manual* (Chicago: American Library Assn., 1995), 3. Another question is "Are students learning what is described in the curriculum objectives of the program?" (p. 6). For a different discussion, see Catherine A. Palomba and Trudy W. Banta, *Assessment Essentials: Planning, Implementing Assessment in Higher Education* (San Francisco: Jossey-Bass, 1999).

36. Bonnie Gratch Lindauer, "Defining and Measuring the Library's Impact on Campuswide Outcomes," *College & Research Libraries* 59, no. 6 (Nov. 1998): 564.

37. For the complex of the designs needed to address such learning outcomes, see Hernon and McClure, *Evaluation and Library Decision Making*, 77–86.

38. Assn. of College and Research Libraries, *Information Literacy Competency Standards for Higher Education* (Chicago: American Library Assn., 2000.)

39. U.S. Office of Management and Budget, "Primer on Performance Measurement" (28 Feb. 1995), 2. Available: ftp://ftp.fedworld.gov/pub/results/primer01.txt. See also Peter H. Rossi, Howard E. Freeman, and Mark W. Lipsey, *Evaluation: A Systematic Approach*, 6th ed. (Thousand Oaks, Calif.: Sage, 1999).

40. U.S. Office of Management and Budget, "Primer on Performance Measurement," 3.

41. Charles R. McClure, "So What Are the Impacts of Networking on Academic Institutions," *Internet Research* 4, no. 2 (summer 1994): 3.

42. Jennifer Abend and Charles R. McClure, "Recent Views on Identifying Impacts from Public Libraries," *Public Library Quarterly* 17, no. 3 (1999): 3–29.

43. See Hernon and Altman, *Assessing Service Quality*, 69 (figure 4.8).

44. "Indiana University Bloomington Libraries Mission and Vision" (Bloomington: Indiana University, 1997). Available: http://www.indiana.edu/~libadmin/mission.html.

45. Wright State University Libraries, "Diversity Vision Statement" (Dayton, Ohio, 1999). Available: http://www.libraries.wright.edu/policies/diversity.html.

46. Freed and Klugman, *Quality Principles and Practices in Higher Education*, 224–33 (appendix C).

47. See Jamie A. Hastreiter, Marsha Cornelius, and David W. Henderson, comps., *Mission Statements for College Libraries*, 2d ed. (Chicago: American Library Assn., Assn. of College and Research Libraries, 1999).

48. University of Maryland Libraries, "Libraries Mission" (College Park, Md.). Available: http://www.lib.umd.edu/UMCP/PUB/mission.html.

49. Letter to Peter Hernon from Ann J. Wolpert, Director of Libraries, Massachusetts Institute of Technology, Cambridge, Mass. (9 Dec. 1999).

50. Suffolk University, Sawyer Library, "Strategic Plan, July 1, 1999–June 30, 2002" (Boston, Mass.: Suffolk University, 1999), 1.

51. "The Mission of a University Undergraduate Library: Model Statement," *College & Research Libraries News* 48, no. 9 (Oct. 1987): 542–4.

52. Madison M. Mosley Jr., "Mission Statements for the Community College LRC," *College & Research Libraries News* 49, no. 10 (Nov. 1988): 653–4.

53. University of North Carolina at Chapel Hill, Health Sciences Library, "Strategic Plan" (revised 1990). Supplied to Hernon from Carol G. Jenkins, Director, 24 Sept. 1990.

54. Stueart and Moran, *Library and Information Center Management*, 58–9, 64.

55. Tony Leisner, "Mission Statements and the Marketing Mix," *Public Libraries* 25, no. 3 (fall 1986): 86–7.

56. See, for instance, "Standards for College Libraries"; "Guidelines for University Undergraduate Libraries," *College & Research Libraries News* 58, no. 5 (May 1997): 330–3; "ACRL Guidelines for Extended Campus Library Services," *College & Research Libraries News* 51, no. 4 (April 1990): 353–5; "Stan-

dards for Community, Junior, and Technical College Learning Resources Program," *College & Research Libraries News* 55, no. 9 (Sept. 1994): 572–85; "Standards for University Libraries: Evaluation of Performance," *College & Research Libraries News* 50, no. 8 (Aug. 1989): 679–91. "The University of Pittsburgh has devised a novel way to try to improve the graduation rates and grades of minority students: Academic deans whose schools fail to bring the rates in line with those of white students will have their budgets cut." See "The University of Pittsburgh," *Academe Today's Daily Report [The Chronicle of Higher Education]* (29 Jan. 1999). Available: http://chronicle.com.

57. Himmel and Wilson, *Planning for Results: The Guidebook*, 58–122.

58. Hernon and Altman, *Service Quality in Academic Libraries*, 157; Hernon and Altman, *Assessing Service Quality*, 147–79.

59. U.S. National Performance Review, *World-Class Courtesy*, section 1.1.

GOALS AND OBJECTIVES
Sawyer Library, Suffolk University

Information Resources

Information resources, owned or assessed, available in a multiplicity of formats, are the most important asset of the Sawyer Library. An academic institution can provide a library staff and a physical facility. However, without information resources, it would not be a library.

The Sawyer Library purchases materials for ownership and availability within the physical facility, primarily in print. Microforms, usually serials, are acquired to save shelf space. Over the past several years the Library has allocated an increasing percentage of its information resources budget to acquire access to materials it does not own through vendors of electronic resources. Access is provided to the Suffolk University community from remote sites as well as within the Library and throughout the campus.

The University will be 100 years old in 2006. University Archives, housed in the Library, will increasingly become a focal point as the expected centennial celebration is considered.

Goal 1

Acquire collections of resources in appropriate formats to meet the information needs of the Library's primary clientele.

Objectives

1.1: Identify the information needs of students, faculty, staff, and administration.
1.2: Create a collection development plan incorporating all formats.

Goal 2

Provide access to unowned resources in appropriate formats to meet the information needs of the Library's primary clientele.

Objectives

2.1: Increase access to and retrieval of information resources in electronic formats for the University community throughout the world.
2.2: Increase our cooperative efforts with other libraries and institutions to expand information services and resource sharing.

Goal 3

Ensure the long-term availability of Library and University archival resources.

Objective

3.1: Develop and implement a plan to preserve those resources determined to be irreplaceable, valuable, unique, or essential because of content, authorship, or format.

Information Services

While information resources are critical to an academic library, the Sawyer Library is further developing its instructional role in assisting students to understand and utilize processes to access and retrieve information. As we increasingly access information not selected in the conventional manner of collection development, the need to provide the University community with the skills to assess and evaluate information sources often remote to the Library also increases.

Employing the appropriate information technologies in the Library for users is becoming more complicated. The availability of the image and sound-based World Wide Web requires computer workstations in place of text-based terminals. Because of the University's policy to not require students to possess their own computer workstations, the Library must continue its role of ensuring opportunities for students to have access to appropriate computer hardware, software, and networking technologies in order to support their information needs based upon course requirements.

Goal 4

The Library's primary clientele will become self-sufficient in information access and retrieval.

Objectives

4.1: Guide the University community to acquire and improve skills in accessing and retrieving information.

4.2: Develop and schedule classes for instruction concerning information access and retrieval on specific products and services for both general applications and subject-specific disciplines.

4.3: Develop means to provide these services to University students remote to the Boston campus.

Goal 5

Employ technologies that support access and retrieval of information, and increase user productivity.

Objectives

5.1: Plan for the expansion and integration of library technologies and services.

5.2: Increase user productivity concerning information access and retrieval.

5.3: Enhance the Library's Web site as the primary mechanism to access electronic resources and information provided/about/created by the Library.

5.4: Support user productivity with computer workstations and software including office suites and e-mail.

Support Structures

Internal support structures are required to provide users with information resources and services. In the case of the Sawyer Library, staff and the physical facility are both mission-critical in supporting information services. Furthermore, the Sawyer Library is not a standalone entity; it is one component of the entire Suffolk University community and must be an active participant in University matters. The Library must manage its allocated resources, access and evaluate its efforts, announce its successes, and seek assistance when needed.

Goal 6

Recruit, foster, and retain a qualified staff to perform those activities necessary to meet the information needs of the Library's primary clientele.

Objectives

6.1: Provide opportunities for individual staff development and education.

6.2: Develop meaningful ways to recognize and reward outstanding staff achievements.

6.3: Periodically review working conditions and identify means for improvement.

6.4: Increase internal communications among staff.

Goal 7

Provide an appropriate study, research, and working environment for collections, users, staff, and services.

Objective

7.1: Improve the conditions of the existing facility.

Goal 8

Assert the Library's role in the University community through active participation.

Objectives

8.1: Participate in University matters by convening, joining, or advising committees regarding activities that may affect Library services.

8.2: Collaborate with University administrators, officials, and others on all procedures, guidelines, and policy decisions affecting the Library.

8.3: Create a public information program to increase awareness of Library services and resources.

Extracted from Suffolk University, Sawyer Library, "Strategic Plan, July 1, 1999–June 30, 2002" (Boston: The Library, 1999).

Public Library Mission Statements

Allen County (Fort Wayne, Indiana) Public Library
http://www.acpl.lib.in.us/about_acpl/index/annual_report.html

> The Library is a service institution. It seeks to inform, educate, entertain, and culturally enrich the entire community by providing books and other library materials, facilities, and professional services for free use by all residents. [Author's note: This statement, although not specifically identified as a mission statement, resembles one.]

Cleveland Public Library
http://www.cpl.org/cpl_mission.html

> The mission of the Cleveland Public Library is to be the best urban library system in the country by providing access to the worldwide information that people and organizations need in a timely, convenient, and equitable manner.

Denver Public Library
http://www.denver.lib.co.us/dpl/aboutpl.html

> The mission of the Denver Public Library is to help the people of our community to achieve their full potential.
>
> > *Actions:* Inform, educate, inspire, entertain
> >
> > *Means:* The printed page, electronic resources, expertise, programs, facilities
> >
> > *Values:* Service, communication, diversity, teamwork, safety, free and equal access to information
> >
> > *Style:* Open, inclusive, friendly, respectful, responsive, confident, innovative, nimble

King County Library System (Seattle, Washington)
http://www.kcls.org/kcls/mission.html

> The mission of the King County Library System is to provide free, open and equal access to ideas and information to all members of the community.
>
> ## PRINCIPLES OF SERVICE
> - Provide open, nonjudgmental access to collections and services without regard to race, citizenship, age, educational level, economic status, religion, or any other qualification or condition;
> - Provide free access to, and promote the communication of, ideas and information;

- Advocate and support First Amendment rights and the Library Bill of Rights, and protect library materials from censorship; and
- Create an environment which encourages users to encounter the rich diversity of concepts on which a democratic society depends.

Los Angeles Public Library
http://www.lapl.org/admin/Mission.html

The Los Angeles Public Library strives to inform, enrich, and empower every individual in its community by creating and promoting free and easy access to a vast array of ideas and information and by supporting lifelong learning in a welcoming environment.

Multnomah County Library (Portland, Oregon)
http://www.multnomah.lib.or.us/lib/about/mcl-mssn.html

Multnomah County Library serves the people of Multnomah County by providing books and other materials to meet their information, education, cultural, and recreational needs.

The Multnomah County Library upholds the principles of intellectual freedom and the public's right to know by providing people of all ages with access and guidance to information and collections that reflect all points of view.

We believe in:

THE PRINCIPLES OF INTELLECTUAL FREEDOM

- We will provide books, programs, and other library resources that present a wide range of views on current and historical issues for the interest, information, and enlightenment of the community;
- We will not exclude materials because of their origin or background or the views they express, nor will we remove materials because of partisan or doctrinal disapproval;
- We will challenge censorship and cooperate with all persons and groups concerned with resisting the abridgment of free expression and free access to ideas;
- We will neither deny nor abridge a person's right to use a library because of his/her age, economic levels, beliefs, race, personal or physical characteristics;
- We will make existing meeting rooms available to the public on an equitable basis; and
- We will ensure regular staff training in the principles of intellectual freedom.

RESPECT FOR THE PUBLIC WE SERVE

Regardless of age, economic level, beliefs, race, personal or physical characteristics:

- We will treat each patron in a courteous and attentive manner;
- We will give all individuals the same consideration and level of service;

- We will see that the library's behavioral rules are upheld in order to make the library a pleasant place for all patrons; and
- We will act in accordance with the intent of library policies and procedures, both in their application and in any exceptions made to them.

EFFECTIVE AND EFFICIENT SERVICE

- We will strive for accuracy and quality in the services we provide;
- We will view all interaction with the public as an opportunity to promote and support the library; and
- We will review and update policies and procedures as needed.

San Francisco Public Library

http://sfpl.ca.us/www/mission_statement.html

The San Francisco Public Library is dedicated to free and equal access to information, knowledge, independent learning, and the joys of reading for our diverse community.

Seattle Public Library

http://spl.lib.wa.us

Our mission is to become the best public library in the world by being so tuned to the people we serve and so supportive of each other's efforts that we are able to provide highly responsive service. We strive to inform, enrich, and empower every person in our community by creating and promoting easy access to a vast array of ideas and information and by supporting an informed citizenry, lifelong learning, and love of reading. We acquire, organize, and provide books and other relevant materials; ensure access to information sources throughout the nation and around the world; serve our public with expert and caring assistance; and reach out to all members of our community.

For the mission statements of other libraries, see St. Joseph County Public Library, "SJCPL's List of Public Libraries with WWW Services" (http://sjcpl.lib.in.us/homepage/PublicLibraries/PublicLibraryServers.html).

WRIGHT STATE UNIVERSITY'S
Commitment to Excellence

The Wright State University Libraries offer the following promises and services to its patrons.

> ┌─ COMMITMENT TO EXCELLENCE ─────────┐
>
> We will provide courteous, prompt, and accurate service to every patron.
>
> We will listen carefully to your needs and respond to them appropriately.
>
> We will do our best to provide resources to meet your research needs.
>
> We will offer opportunities for instruction about our resources and services.
>
> We will provide an environment that is conducive to study and research.
>
> We will not give you the runaround. We will provide the assistance you need, or we will put you in contact with someone who can.

GENERAL SERVICES

- Provide users with the tools and training to enable access to the University Libraries' collection and to resources available nationally.
- Publicize changes in our services and provide opportunities for training for new services.
- Maintain designated quiet study areas.
- Provide a clean and comfortable study environment.

REFERENCE AND INSTRUCTION

- Provide professional reference assistance to help patrons use the Libraries' collections and resources.
- Assist faculty by developing instructional presentations tailored to the needs of a class.
- Provide reference and instructional support for faculty for specific assignments.

COLLECTION DEVELOPMENT

- Ensure that the Libraries' collections support the instructional and research mission of Wright State University and maintain the reliability of the LIBNET* system (including the provision of workstations capable of efficient printing and/or downloading).
- Catalog materials accurately and promptly.

- Make new books available within four weeks of receipt and provide rush delivery when necessary.
- Locate acceptable substitutes immediately or provide copies within 48 hours when requested materials are at the bindery.
- Respond to faculty book orders within five working days.
- Review academic needs with university departments every academic quarter.

INFORMATION DELIVERY

- Check out and check in all books and materials accurately.
- Place interlibrary loan requests within two days.
- Shelve current periodicals within 24 hours of receipt.
- Reshelve books and bound periodicals within 24 hours of use.
- Reshelve current periodicals within one hour of use.
- Initiate searches for missing materials.

SPECIAL COLLECTIONS

- Offer personalized assistance for patron research needs.
- Locate materials housed on-site within five minutes.
- Complete photocopies of special collection materials within 48 hours.
- Respond to in-person, telephone, and electronic mail queries.

Wright State University Libraries, "Commitment to Excellence" (Dayton, Ohio, 1999).
Available: http://www.libraries.wright.edu/services/Customer_Services.html.

*LIBNET is the gateway to the Wright State University Libraries and to OhioLINK resources.

5 Developing and Implementing a Service Plan

It is up to librarians and their staffs to demonstrate the value of libraries to everyone in their community—not just a select few, not even just those who enter their doors, but everyone! This focus on customer service applies not just to public librarians, but to school, college and special librarians as well. Together, we must rededicate ourselves to our mission of customer service, to reaching out to diverse people and to providing the types of service that will raise their hopes, help them solve problems and achieve their aspirations.[1]

The library's mission plays the guiding role in fulfilling its vision. The mission is achieved by a set of stated goals, which, in turn, are further refined by a set of objectives, the implementation of which can be measured. These goals and objectives—perhaps stated, in part, in the form of a service pledge (see chapter 4)—can lay the basis for setting explicit expectations in the minds of library staff and customers. These expectations will be key to aligning the resources of the library toward their fulfillment, and thus satisfying—indeed delighting—customers.

The Service Plan

A *service plan* is an explicit plan to accomplish the service goals and objectives set by the library's mission. There may be nonservice goals (having to do with facilities and other dimensions of the library's plant or operations), but these come into play only insofar as they pertain to the desired delivery of service to satisfy the customer.

As Susan Wehmeyer, Dorothy Auchter, and Arnold Hirshon described in chapter 4, the service plan involves the solicitation of customer feedback in multiple ways, both continuously and at designated times of the year, the orientation or training of employees, and the actions of top management to ensure that service delivery improvements are made specifically in response to customer indications.[2] The service plan, as described in this chapter, however, goes deeper and farther. It calls for taking control of the factors that influence service quality and satisfaction, setting customer expectations, and hiring staff who are aligned with the library's customer mission and empowering them to deliver outstanding service. The entire plan can be launched on the basis of an articulated pledge to customers that is drawn up in a way that involves the entire staff.

Goals and Objectives

The first criterion for designing a service plan is to have explicit goals and objectives not only in mind but on paper. The goals represent the state to be achieved following implementation of one or more objectives. One form of measurement is bipolar: the goal or objective is achieved or it is not achieved. Indeed, it is a challenge for public service organizations to define such bipolar goals and objectives. William D. Ruckelshaus, the first administrator of the U.S. Environmental Protection Agency (EPA), recognized this immediately when he had to determine the goals for the EPA when it was founded.

> There was a need to establish for the agency some clear goals that everybody could identify with. I went around and talked to a lot of them in the agency. . . .
> I looked at the two most recent examples of agencies like EPA: OEO [Office of Equal Opportunity] and NASA [National Aeronautics and Space Administration]. I looked at them in terms of what their statutory goals were. NASA's had been very narrowly defined, in terms of "let's get to the moon in ten years," and they achieved it. . . . OEO, on the other hand, had a very amorphous goal: "let's do something about poverty." Some would say that is what they were doing: *something* about poverty. This was the kind of progress that is very difficult to measure.
>
> I felt that *we* had to be very careful that EPA did not go to either of those extremes. So, we defined our initial goal as pollution abatement. This was fairly narrow, in the environmental sense, but nevertheless it was identifiable enough, understandable enough, to let us know what we were doing, so that we could move towards the goal.[3]

What Ruckelshaus sensed was the need for goals that were neither bipolar nor amorphous. He employed a more refined type of goal based on being able to measure degrees of attainment, which, in turn, were expressed as measurable objectives. For example, instead of insisting on the unacceptably costly (and perhaps impractical) attainment of zero pollution, the EPA formulates compliance based on acceptable thresholds of tolerance, such as a pollutant level not exceeding so many parts per billion. This scalable form of measurable outcome is pertinent to customer satisfaction as well.

It is not adequate to state merely that the library will satisfy customers, suggesting that customers can be either satisfied or not satisfied. It is much more reasonable and attainable to state that the library (using periodic surveys to measure attainment) will achieve an average customer satisfaction score of at least 8, on a scale of 1 to 10, for overall satisfaction and for each of the dimensions of service offered to customers. Moreover, it can be stated that the library will consider overall satisfaction scores of 4 or below to be unacceptable, indicating that a failure to deliver satisfaction occurred in such cases, and that such cases should account for no more than, for example, 5 percent of responses. Once a set of goals and objectives that allows one to measure whether the library's service mission is being achieved is drafted, the next step is to articulate these goals and objectives by creating for them a set of specific and explicit expectations to be met.

To the extent that satisfaction is a function of expectations, and that different customers may have different expectations of service delivery, customers are likely to rate satisfaction differently. This may or may not be desirable. It means that achieving satisfaction is left open to the widely different sets of conscious and unconscious expectations that different people bring with them to the library, which poses the challenge of satisfying different and possibly mutually exclusive expectations.

Consider how much simpler it would be to satisfy customers who shared a common set of expectations, especially if those expectations were clearly established by the library whose personnel were aligned to meet those expectations. Greater control over the outcome is possible if it is made clear what expectations customers *should* have and that the library (meaning everyone involved in service delivery) intends to meet these specific expectations. To the extent that the library is successful in setting and communicating this set of expectations—and through consistent service delivery is able to meet (or exceed) these expectations—the library has far more control over delivering a satisfying experience to customers who, otherwise, have different prior experiences and expectations.

Moreover, with a clearly defined set of expectations for service delivery, everyone, including library staff, now has a common understanding of the minimum acceptable level of service delivery. This vastly reduces the likelihood that different staff members will be delivering service according to their respective concepts of what is acceptable; now they have an objective standard to achieve.

This is not to say that all customers must have identical expectations. For example, a public library can define one set of expectations for customers who use the library for reference purposes and another set for those who use the library for finding children's books. Further, the art of setting expectations can, in some cases, mean setting explicit boundaries of service so that the customer will not have expectations that cannot be met. An obvious example of this is clearly informing customers of library weekend hours, thus discouraging customers from arriving at a closed library. The key point is for the library to define customer expectations that can be met for those services the library intends to deliver (see chapter 2) and to deliver well.

The service plan is not cast in bronze; it is adjustable. It may prove impossible, impractical, or, for some reason, undesirable to attempt a stated goal or objective as originally planned. This can be discovered through feedback from customers and staff. The inappropriate goal or objective is then modified or abandoned and perhaps replaced by a more reasonable or pertinent one. Perhaps a new opportunity to deliver service is discovered, so this is added to the service plan. The service plan is itself a dynamic, organic process that evolves according to choices and opportunities made explicit through a satisfaction and service-quality relationship that has been put in place involving the staff and customers.

So far, the discussion has focused on service delivery as if only library staff have a role to play in achieving expectations. This need not be the case. The customer also has a role to play. By setting expectations in the customer's mind, the library is taking control of the ability to provide satisfactory service. The customer also needs to be informed of what to expect and of how to take advantage of the full range of services offered. In exchange, the customer should be asked to rate from time to time how the library is doing and what, if anything, the customer would like that is not yet being offered. In other words, a relationship can be established with the customer that offers an active role for the customer to help define and assess the service delivered. This is the *satisfaction relationship* illustrated in figure 3.3.

The same conceptual framework for defining a satisfaction relationship with the customer can now be applied to library staff. The process begins by setting explicit expectations for service performance as it pertains to the job of each staff member. This is combined with a request that each staff member report, from time to time, how satisfying the job is and how the job can be improved. Not incidentally, the person can also share insights into how he or she (or others in the library) can improve service to the customer. This framework, the employee-satisfaction nexus (see figure 3.4), provides far more agreeable control over staff expectations, creating a satisfactory work environment and improving the employee's ability to provide service to library customers. This integrated framework of relationships—with the satisfaction relationship defined as a dynamic interchange of setting expectations, delivering service to meet or exceed these expectations, and getting feedback on performance and what could be improved—becomes the service plan.

Steps of the Service Plan

The relationships that describe the service plan must be turned into action. Six steps mobilize the service plan:

1. Take control of the factors that influence service quality and satisfaction.

2. Set expectations for customers based on what can be delivered.

3. Define the relationship between the customer and the library.

4. Empower employees to satisfy customers.

5. Ask for feedback by, for instance, using special questionnaires and forms.

6. Respond to customers individually and collectively.

Take Control

The concept of taking control refers to the process of understanding the factors that influence how service quality and satisfaction are defined, achieved, and assessed and how these factors influence the mission of the library and its funding. It also refers to the process of using one's management prerogatives and skills in taking control of elements within one's domain and power in order to influence outcomes.

Figure 5.1, which arranges a set of relationships called "the wheel of influence," illustrates the key interrelating factors. In this model, the *funding source* is placed at the top. This source will vary in libraries of different types, but in all cases the funding source will be the individual or body that is responsible for allocating the library budget or has ultimate responsibility for how much money the library is given to operate according to its mission. This is the group that has its hands on the purse strings. In a public library, this group is the board of trustees or local government; in an academic library, it may be the provost and others who allocate the budget. From the funding source, follow the wheel counterclockwise.

The next point of influence is the *mission* itself. Clearly, those individuals who are charged with the funding responsibility significantly influence the acceptance, if not the definition, of the mission. The connection between the funding source and the mission is integral.

Continuing counterclockwise past the mission, the next influence point is *execution*. This represents all the ways in which the library's mission is carried out and, in particular, the ways in which service is delivered to the customer. Some service can be delivered to the customer without necessarily involving staff directly; however, the role of staff in delivering service to customers is critical. This link between staff and customer is reforged each time an inter-

FIGURE 5.1
The Wheel of Influence

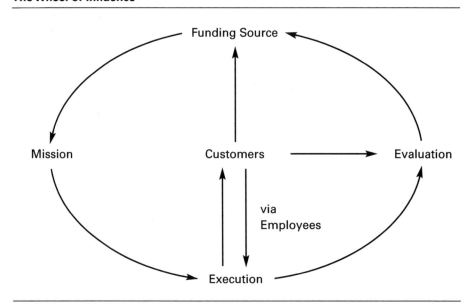

action between the two takes place, and it is through such encounters that the customer creates a mental image of the library and its panoply of offerings. Jan Carlzon describes such encounters as "moments of truth."[4] This link is so important that it appears in greater detail in figure 3.4.

The next point of influence is *evaluation*, which denotes the process by which service delivery to the customer is assessed and judged in relation to whether, and to what degree, the mission is being accomplished. The results of this evaluation, in turn, may influence the funding source, either by confirming that the intended mission is being achieved with the designated budget or by signaling that some action may be required to accomplish the mission better (or that the mission itself may need to be revised).

With the wheel of influence model in mind, one can now visualize the key points over which control can be exercised for the model to work in an optimal manner. The placement of customers inside the wheel of influence indicates the central role that they play in both execution (as the recipients of library services) and evaluation (as providing an assessment of how satisfied they are with the execution). Customers can also influence the funding source directly simply by initiating a contact by phone, mail, e-mail, or by some other means, though this is an option over which the library management has little or no control.

For the sake of simplicity, other factors of influence are missing from figure 5.1, including, for instance, factors that may influence or even control the funding body, such as the role of the press and stakeholders, and competitive factors that offer alternatives to customers. For the sake of simplicity, this model focuses on the more immediate factors over which library management can exercise control.

In summary, it is advantageous to set customer expectations that the library can realistically meet (or preferably exceed). By doing so, the library establishes not only a frame of reference for the customer's relationship but also an objective reference that orients the staff and that indicates whether the library is satisfactorily achieving service delivery. Furthermore, the library establishes a foundation on which it can build.

Set Expectations

Most customers have some set of preconceived notions of what they expect from a library. Most, however, have probably not thought very much about their expectations and probably would not do so unless and until some kind of *satisfaction surprise* takes place. An event that significantly deviates from expectations is a satisfaction surprise. When something unexpectedly nice takes place for customers, they are happy and pleased. When a particular book that has been requested through interlibrary loan for eight weeks still has not materialized or an otherwise untoward event jolts their sensibilities, however, customers who are usually satisfied can suddenly become very unhappy and express their displeasure to friends and colleagues.

In the case of commercial enterprises, an untoward service surprise, otherwise known as a *service failure*, can have a severely damaging effect on reputation, and too many businesses respond to such events poorly. Although such service failures do not occur often, they can seem unavoidable in certain cases, such as accidentally spilled food or a drink at a restaurant. How the business responds can make or break its reputation with the affected customer and have a ripple effect through word of mouth. A standout response in the case of service failure can do wonders to maintain and even enhance a business's reputation. Key to managing service failures is having a plan for recovering from them when they occur.

Service failures can occur in libraries as well. As previously discussed, the library management can determine that any satisfaction score below a defined threshold (e.g., 4 on a 10-point scale) signifies a service failure and should warrant immediate corrective action. In fact, by the time such a failure shows up on a satisfaction survey (if it does so at all), it may be too late to correct. The library's service plan should, therefore, instruct staff about how to respond to service failures as they occur.

The library that can explicitly define its customers' expectations is in a much better position to please them. In effect, the library is stating, "Here is what we are going to do for you," and then making good (or better) on the promise. This approach to defining and setting customer expectations is a fundamental part of the described strategy to *create* service quality and customer satisfaction.

Library staff, with leadership from management, can determine specific expectations worthy of attention and include these expectations as part of a service pledge (see chapter 4, appendix B). They might also review chapter 2 and various service dimensions, selecting the most important ones and executing these especially well. A *dimension* is a measurable attribute or feature of the service operation. *Measurable* means that a customer would be able to rate these dimensions from poor to excellent. A list of dimensions (see question 6 in figures 6.2 and 6.3 for examples of dimensions) relates to

> products and their information content (e.g., accuracy, relevance, and understandability)
>
> the service environment (e.g., physical surroundings; service reputation; redress for receiving poor service; and the availability and accessibility of information, facilities, and equipment)
>
> service delivery provided by staff (e.g., the speed of delivery, staff behavior, and assistance provided)[5]

A library might select some dimensions that relate to its specialty and uniqueness. For example, a historical map collection may distinguish a library, and it might be important to list this dimension first (e.g., "The historical map collection . . . "). A list of ten to fifteen dimensions would be reasonable to include. The total number of dimensions should not exceed twenty because respondents may tire from considering such a number of items and the quality of their responses may diminish.

It is critical to identify dimensions that are most valuable to customers and that the library can deliver especially well. Measuring a dimension that is not perceived to be of value to customers does little if any good. Furthermore, it is not advised to include dimensions that the library is not in a position to improve. For example, unless the library is in a position to improve a poor parking situation, having customers rate parking may only raise their expectations that the situation will be improved. In any case, customers who feel a dimension that is important to them is missing from the list are likely to add it to the list themselves or reference it through their comments.

To help identify dimensions, the staff might interview a few customers or conduct one or more focus group interviews with customers to get their perspectives. According to William H. Davidow and Bro Uttal, "All too many companies, when developing customer services, never bother asking customers what they expect."[6] Unless a set of expectations is already clear, it may help to talk to customers to find out in their own words what they expect from the library. It can also be enlightening to ask them what sets the library apart from other libraries and from other competing organizations.

As indicated earlier, a carefully selected list of service dimensions will become crucial to telling customers what they can expect from the library. The point is to establish expectations by making clear what can—and will—be guaranteed. Once a list of dimensions is drawn up, the goal is to select those that the library is prepared to meet. Other dimensions, however, might be chosen for priority attention later or for an explanation of why the library is not prepared to meet them.

Making expectations explicit to the customer is a form of educating the customer. The intent is to prepare the customer for how to make the best use of the library's services. Such an educational approach can go further than setting expectations by anticipating problems that have arisen in the past and by providing customers with information on how to avoid such problems in the future. It can be instructive to ask, for example, whether customers have been dissatisfied because of a misunderstanding about how to use the library's services or a lack of knowledge about the existence of, or limitations to, its services. If such cases can be identified, it may be helpful to compile a list of "If only the customer knew" items. Figure 5.2 provides an example of such a list. This list can be an extension of the effort to set customer expectations and to avoid or minimize service failures. The list could be included in a library newsletter, in a write-up for a local or campus newspaper, or in a handout available at the circulation and reference departments.

Define the Relationship

The key enforcement element in the shift from the transaction relationship to the satisfaction relationship is the service guarantee. By now the customers' expectations in terms of service dimensions have been set. The next step is to enforce, or back up, the intention to deliver these expectations with a clearly and simply worded message or pledge to customers: satisfaction guaranteed.

A guarantee of satisfaction is the acid test of the commitment to quality. Guarantees are easy to understand, manage, and measure. The form of the guarantee in a business setting offers some latitude and flexibility not typically found in libraries. In a business, unsatisfied or dissatisfied customers usually expect some form of financial redress, typically a rebate or refund. In this sense, the guarantee acts as a form of self-imposed enforcement, with a financial penalty exacted when failure occurs. Because the form of

FIGURE 5.2
Sample "If Only the Customer Knew" List

Do you know that

- the library offers free workshops on how to use the Internet? (Ask the front desk for a schedule of courses.)
- the library is open extra late on Friday evenings, until 10 P.M.?
- you can reserve a book without visiting the library by using the Internet?
- you can see the entire library catalog on your computer at home?
- the library can order any book you want from the entire metropolitan library network?
- the hall on the lower level now offers coffee and snack machines?
- the library offers literacy programs on Saturday mornings?
- you can drop off books outside the main entrance at any time, day or night?
- you can borrow most videos at no cost and can borrow selected, recent videos for only $2?
- you can request the library to purchase a specific book, video, or CD for its collection?
- you can ask a reference librarian to help you find what you need?
- you can report your satisfaction or dissatisfaction with library service to the library director by using the Customer Satisfaction Questionnaire or the Service Improvement Form? (Both are available at the reference and circulation desks.)

---

redress is usually a financial one, this affords the business owner options in the form of the redress, the amount to compensate, the refund timing, and so forth. In a library, where money rarely changes hands directly, what practical form can a guarantee assume?

Without a direct analog to financial redress, libraries thereby lack a useful management tool because the enforcement effect of a financial penalty is a powerful motivator, and the absence of such motivation can lead to erratic performance. Perhaps the next best thing to a financial penalty for a service failure is, therefore, the opportunity to report dissatisfaction directly to top management.

This is a key function of the compliment/complaint system as discussed in *Assessing Service Quality*, the customer satisfaction questionnaires, and the service improvement report (see chapter 6).[7] Whenever a problem occurs, the staff should, of course, take remedial action to resolve the problem. (The library management must define in advance what constitutes a service failure and the extent to which employees can exercise their own discretion in resolving the matter or should seek management assistance in responding.) In addition, the customer should be invited (without pressure) to complete a form to report the incident. Alternatively, any library staff member may also report the problem. There should be a system or procedure for reviewing the forms and determining why failures occurred. The key is to treat these episodes as lessons learned—opportunities to identify and correct problems.

It is simple to keep track of the number, percentage, and stated causes of service failures identified as indicators of how well the library is doing. In fact, gauging the number of service failures that are likely to occur in the course of a fiscal year can help determine how much should be allocated to recover from these failures. This analysis is worth conducting. If, for example, a large number of complaints arise concerning books missing from their places in the stacks, it may be appropriate to allocate greater staff time to returning books to the shelves in a more timely manner or if the books are, in fact, missing, to consider their possible replacement.

Empower Employees

The service plan includes a central role—indeed, a critical role—for staff. The employee-satisfaction nexus (see figure 3.4) describes the opportunity to create a culture in the library in which every staff member becomes committed to service quality and customer satisfaction, knows how to deliver both, and is empowered to do so. Too often, support staff are merely thrust into their jobs without adequate orientation and training. Starting and maintaining an ongoing dialog with staff that makes them feel part of a team approach to delivering service quality and customer satisfaction, beginning with employees' first days on the job, can prove pivotal in ensuring mission success. The service plan offers two ways to align staff to deliver customer satisfaction: hiring right, and repeated orientation (or, more formally, training).

Hiring right refers to the way in which the library presents employment opportunities to job candidates and describes what is expected from them, in terms of both their technical qualifications and their motivation to satisfy customers. Clearly, the first step in hiring right is knowing what to look for in a candidate. Richard E. Luce, director of the Research Library of the Los Alamos National Laboratory, describes some of the features sought in a job candidate.

> In addition to whatever technical skills are specific to a given position, we look for the following in hiring new employees:
>
> - Passion for service excellence;
> - People skills (warm, friendly, along with strong communication skills);
> - Self-motivated, lifelong learner;
> - Collaborative, team player;
> - Initiative (takes risks, solves problems); and
> - Flexibility and enthusiasm.[8]

In addition to making clear what is being sought in a candidate, hiring right also refers to the process of screening candidates. Each candidate should be interviewed by more than one library staff member to determine the candidate's skills at interaction with multiple people. Subsequently the interviewers can discuss among themselves how well the candidate might fit into the culture of customer satisfaction and service quality at the library. Additionally, there might be questions about his or her ability to deal well with customers and to deliver service with alacrity.

Many library managers may not be in a position to hire employees of their choice, perhaps because they are required to utilize existing staff within a larger institution. Whether or not the library can conduct its own hiring, its service plan should include an orientation or training program for new and existing staff in which the library management sets explicit expectations for service delivery and customer satisfaction, instructs staff about how to deliver outstanding service, and offers examples of how to respond to and recover from service failures. The orientation program should include a presentation on the library's mission, how achieving the mission requires delivery of the services offered by the library, how the library sets customer expectations for service delivery and surveys customers for service quality and satisfaction, and the results of the most recent service quality and satisfaction surveys, including how management took action to resolve any problems that may have come to light as a result of a survey. Finally, the orientation program should provide all employees with an opportunity to provide management with their own insights on and suggestions about how to deliver and improve satisfaction as well as any possible need they may express for additional resources that would further empower them to deliver outstanding service. Such an orientation program should be repeated from time to time, annually or biannually, depending on staff turnover and the need to align or realign staff.

The result of hiring right and repeated orientation will be a staff that is rowing together with the customers' expectations in mind. They will understand how satisfaction relates to the library's mission, and they will be able to demonstrate their role in providing service knowing that they are empowered—indeed challenged—to deliver satisfaction.

Ask for Feedback

The service plan, so far, has focused on ways for the library to set the table for service delivery. The actual delivery takes place on a daily basis. Monitoring how well service is, in fact, being delivered requires one or more feedback loops in which customers can report how well they are being served, with their reports being delivered to top management at the library. Such feedback can take place in several informal as well as formal ways.

Informally, the library director can engage in "management by walking around." Informal and unscheduled observations of the various service-delivery points, combined with spontaneous and unobtrusive conversation with staff and customers, can deliver a wealth of information. By asking direct questions, such as "How is everything going?" or "Are you getting the assistance or support you need?," directors may discover something that, otherwise, might have gone unnoticed.

Asking questions in informal settings is only one way to acquire the desired feedback. Two additional methods of soliciting feedback are to conduct a satisfaction survey and to use a service improvement reporting form. The satisfaction survey is a periodic—perhaps annual—invitation to customers asking them to report how well the library is delivering services and to identify areas that need attention. The service improvement reporting form, or a comment card (as described in *Assessing Service Quality*), can be completed by customers or staff at any time throughout the year.[9]

Customer suggestions reported on either instrument may include ideas for improving service. When such a suggestion is implemented in a way that could have an impact on satisfaction, it is called a "change event." Keeping a record of these change events—and if they indeed affect satisfaction—may, over time, reveal why the satisfaction score is rising, falling, or staying the same after the date of the change event. Some change events may result in falling satisfaction scores. Taking note of the date that a downward trend begins may provide a clue about a possible change in service delivery (or some other environmental change) that may be related to a greater degree of dissatisfaction.

As an example, suppose that in response to customer requests, a library places a book return box in the parking lot, thereby making it more convenient for customers to return books. Satisfaction with the dimension involving book returns falls precipitously in a subsequent survey, however. Reading the comments section, it becomes clear that dissatisfied customers are complaining that the book return in the parking lot is consistently full when they need it most and that books consequently stack up on the asphalt and sustain weather damage. An investigation discovers that the staff find it inconvenient to collect the books from the parking lot, particularly in inclement weather, which is exactly when such a book drop is most convenient to customers.

The customer satisfaction and/or service quality survey process will not prove that a change event is actually causing a change in customer satisfaction one way or the other. Given the context, however, it may be reasonable to infer that a change event has resulted in a change in customer satisfaction. Business people make such inferences on a daily basis. They know that they develop certain impressions and make certain decisions based on incomplete data and information, and they know that it is rare to be completely certain that they have enough information on which to make decisions. But decide they do, even when the picture is incomplete. In fact, if they waited to compose a complete picture of every situation, they might lose valuable time and opportunity.

It is important to distinguish between two types of possible surveys to measure customer satisfaction. In one type of survey—a *research survey*—the goal is to determine as exactly as possible the true satisfaction score for a known population of current or possible library users. The appropriate approach to conducting such a survey would be to undertake either a census, in which all members of the population take part in responding, or a scientifically selected sample survey, in which a random sample of the population is taken as a means to estimate the true population mean score. In the second type of survey—a *management survey*—data are collected from a rather loosely defined sample of the population. This approach should include a large enough number of participants to get a very general picture of the level of satisfaction and, perhaps more important, to identify specific areas of service delivery that may require improvement. The management reason for conducting such a survey is not to know an exact average satisfaction score for the entire population but to improve the delivery of library services in ways designed to increase overall satisfaction. The purpose of this book is to focus on employing the latter approach as a management tool. Certainly, a research survey could be undertaken; however, the utility of the management survey approach is enhanced by the fact that one need not be trained in survey research or statistics to benefit significantly from the process.

A survey approach is not a substitute for all the other reality checks required to run a library and make critical and timely decisions. In the last analysis, no matter what survey data show, it is up to the senior managers to use business judgment, discretion, and qualities of leadership in deciding how meaningful a picture emerges and how to respond.

Both informal and formal feedback methods are part of the service plan, but it may be tempting to forgo the formal methods if the sense is strong that management already knows what customers think from "walking around" and being close to and talking with customers. This is a sentiment shared among many small business owners who themselves frequently interact with their customers and see no need for the bother of conducting a formal survey. Yet, not all customers are comfortable with sharing their concerns face-to-face with the individual who is in the best position to improve things for them. The formality, distance, and, in many cases, anonymity of the survey process allows customers to be forthright and candid. This assurance to the customer can provide important feedback to management. Finally, what if the survey is conducted only to reveal nothing new? Was the survey a wasted effort? On the contrary, if the survey had not been conducted, how could one be sure? With the hard evidence provided by a survey in hand, management is in a far stronger position to take advantage of opportunities or to make corrections.

Respond to Customers

Customers need to be addressed collectively as a group and, in some cases, individually. They have agreed to respond to the survey, and some have done so after exercising considerable thought. What they have chosen to report is, in their mind, valuable. In some cases, what they say, or how they say it, may be distasteful. It is important, however, to respond to them in order to continue and strengthen the library's relationship with them.

While most forms will be returned unsigned, every customer who has written a meaningful entry for an open-ended question and identifies herself or himself deserves a response. This means sending a note of thanks or placing a telephone call to tell these customers that their comments were received and appreciated. If a call is placed but the customer is absent, leaving a message that the library called to thank them should suffice.

In addition, a presentation based on the survey results should be posted for all in the library to see. This can take the form of a poster in the lobby or reading room, an article in the library newsletter or community newspaper, or a posting on the library's Web site. The point is to share the results of the study with the customers. If appropriate, the report can include the specific steps that are planned to respond to specific issues raised in the survey. This way of sharing the results will let customers know that they did not respond to the survey in vain, and thus they may be much more inclined to respond to the next survey as well.

As previously mentioned, the survey results should be shared with staff both by posting results and by discussing them in orientation sessions and in departmental meetings, as this is a feedback loop for their benefit as well. It may be appropriate to prepare a more formal report for stakeholders and even the local media.

Marketing through Survey Reports

Releasing a survey report is intended to build community support for the conduct of future surveys and to show the broader community that the library prizes feedback from its customers. Library managers might make an informal presentation of survey results as well as post them in public spaces for review by interested customers. Addressing stakeholders and the local media will require a more formal presentation and additional thought and anticipation about what the expectations of these various groups might be, how they might use the information, and what types of questions they may raise about the results and their implications.

Preliminary Considerations

Often upon completion of a survey, one or more interested parties will request a "report" on the findings. Normally, the type of survey described in this book does not require a reporting component (beyond the suggested posting of results), principally because the effort is initiated internally and is intended primarily for consumption by internal management. Had the project been externally requested and possibly externally funded as well, a report would be in order. Nevertheless, it behooves management to anticipate that outside interests may want more details of the project and its results.

Regardless of the specific party showing interest, one should be prepared for more than mere curiosity. A library's governing board may be concerned with the overall management of the library, and it may garner any available data that can be used to judge performance, perhaps as part of a cost-benefit analysis. These considerations are particularly relevant during a time of scarce resources for libraries and other cultural enterprises. The local media, always looking for timely news of interest, might wish to focus on the survey and its results as grist for a story they can present to their audiences.

The Survey Report

Generally speaking, two types of presentations are common in survey research. The first consists of an oral presentation to the interested parties and may not include any written materials, or no more than a set of key points, usually set forth in outline format. The second is a fairly complete document that contains a description of the project as well as the findings and can include as appendixes a substantial set of support material. In certain cases, it may be appropriate to provide the actual database of responses on diskette or in a file transmitted electronically, as long as there is no identification of individual respondents. The purpose of doing so would be to let the recipients conduct further analyses. Following is an outline for a comprehensive report. The components of the report are

executive summary

introduction

background

methodology

results

discussion

recommendations

appendixes

    the questionnaire

    the database structure

    detailed methodology

    data analysis

Executive Summary

The executive summary is a one- or two-page synopsis of the survey and its key findings. The primary information includes the purpose of the survey (unless the survey was a scientifically conducted inferential survey, it should be clearly stated that the results represent only the respondents to the survey and that no statistical inferences can be drawn for nonrespondents), the dates of its execution, the number of people surveyed, and the number of respondents. Following this, the major findings are typically presented as bulleted points, each followed by a one-line statement of the finding. An additional one or two lines per finding may provide supporting information, but brevity is the essence of the summary. This summary may be optional if a more complete document is prepared, or a separate summary may be prepared for different audiences. Such a summary could be included as the first section of a larger document, or it could be distributed by itself. It is important to indicate the name and telephone number of the person who can be contacted for further information and the date that the summary was prepared.

Introduction

The introduction should be one or two pages in length and should describe the purpose and scope of the survey project (the previous caveat regarding who the results represent should be repeated here), the sponsors of the project, who undertook the principal role(s) in conducting the project, and who should be contacted for further information.

Background

The background should be one to three pages long and should present any relevant background to the project, including reference to any previous surveys.

Methodology

The methodology should outline, in two to three pages, the survey process and should include the dates for each step in the process, the number of people surveyed, the number of respondents, the return rate, and any other pertinent information that would describe how the project was conducted. Note that a complete recording of the methodology should be appended.

Results

The results section should set forth each of the findings, including the complete question as it appeared on the questionnaire, the results of the analysis, and any relevant tables or graphs. Each finding should include the number of respondents to the question as well as the percentages for each possible response.

Discussion

This optional section would include the evaluation of the assessment findings. It would also describe any problems that might have occurred during the project that may have affected its outcome or may have influenced how people responded. It might also include notes on what might be done differently should the survey be repeated. These notes can prove quite valuable in the future, whether or not the same personnel are involved in planning and executing the survey.

Recommendations

The recommendations, which are also optional, may be varied, depending on the intended audience of the report. It may be necessary to determine in advance how the report might be used prior to preparing specific recommendations.

Appendixes

The following are the most important appendixes to include with the comprehensive survey report. Depending on the audience, these appendixes may be unnecessary; however, they certainly should be part of the archival report.

THE QUESTIONNAIRE A copy of the complete questionnaire should be included with the report. If the questionnaire was mailed with a cover letter, a copy of the cover letter should be included. In cases of an e-mail or Web survey, printed copies of the message and the HTML form should be included.

THE DATABASE STRUCTURE If a statistical package is used to analyze the data, it is often valuable to include a copy of the database structure and the structure of any tables used by the statistical package. A copy of the database itself should be kept on a diskette and included with the archival copy. The exact name and version of the statistical package(s) used should also be logged and noted on the diskette.

DETAILED METHODOLOGY This appendix should include a complete description of the methodology used to conduct the survey. An independent researcher should be able to replicate the project fully by following the procedures documented in this section.

DATA ANALYSIS The data analysis section should include a complete set of all analyses conducted that support the report, including the software package name and version number used to generate the analysis. This section can be quite large and can fill several binders. Typically, it is not feasible to generate all possible permutations of the analytical possibilities, nor is it advised. Only the pertinent analyses that support the findings should be included.

The Press Release

The press release represents an opportunity for the library to put a success story in front of the local media. It should be written in a manner appropriate for the ultimate audience, which may be the general public or members of a university campus.

The press release can be prepared on the library's letterhead, with block letters at the top of the page indicating that the document is a PRESS RELEASE or NEWS RELEASE, along with the date that the material is authorized for release to the public. The name and telephone number of a library representative who is available for possible contact by the press should also be included. Typically, a press release is no more than two pages in length. The media may appreciate a black-and-white photograph of the library, preferably with customers visible in the picture but with their faces not showing (unless the library has already gained their consent).

The title of the release should be short and interesting, for instance:

Library Stacks up Satisfaction Record

The body of the text typically opens with the name of the academic institution or the city or town, followed by a colon, and the first line of text. The who, what, when, where, why, and how of journalism can apply here, though not necessarily in that order. Following the first one or two paragraphs, which should include the most interesting findings, it is customary to include a quotation attributed to the library director. In addition to, or in lieu of, a quote from the director, it could be interesting to include one or more quotations from actual respondents, for example, in response to a question about what the customer likes best about the library. The balance of the story provides further details and can mention a contact person at the close for those interested in finding out more.

Once the press release is prepared, it should be sent directly to the editors of the target media. In some cases, media firms will accept stories sent by e-mail, but this should not be the assumed format for delivery.

Opportunities for Rewards

For those libraries that are further motivated to achieve professional recognition, there is the possibility of reward in areas where such attention is paid. For example, the Research Library of the Los Alamos National Laboratory applied for a Quality New Mexico Award, involving self-assessment based on the Malcolm Baldrige National Quality Award, and won the Roadrunner Award in 1997. This award recognizes the library for "significant progress in building sound and notable processes through their commitment and implementation of quality principles."[10]

Summary

Developing and implementing a service plan for satisfying customers should be an important responsibility of top management in libraries of all types. An appropriately designed plan can easily be undertaken without the addition of specially skilled personnel and can result in a measurable improvement of service. This chapter defined the framework of, and steps involved in implementing, a service plan that encompasses and exceeds the description of such a plan presented by Wehmeyer, Auchter, and Hirshon. The steps are

1. taking control by understanding the factors of influence and setting goals and (measurable) objectives of service delivery

2. setting expectations by defining the standards of service delivery to meet customer expectations in defined dimensions

3. defining the relationship by issuing to customers a statement that they will be satisfied, backed up by the opportunity to report dissatisfaction as well as satisfaction directly to top management

4. empowering employees by issuing a policy and procedure to inform them of expected standards of service delivery, providing orientation on how to satisfy customers, and giving employees the opportunity to rate their own satisfaction on the job and to report ways to increase customer satisfaction

5. asking for feedback through periodic surveys that allow customers and employees to rate satisfaction and through the use of a form to report a service incident at any time

6. responding to customers by developing a system for reporting back to customers and employees the results of satisfaction studies as well as paying individual attention to particularly low satisfaction experiences

Understood and applied correctly, these steps can be incrementally woven into the management process in a way that should indeed strengthen management control, clarify the role of staff in delivering satisfaction, build a more supportive customer constituency, provide objective data with which to justify needed resources, and ameliorate or eliminate emerging problems that could, if not managed properly, result in far greater costs in resources and time. Moreover, by listening to customer expectations, the library can evolve its mission, stay competitive, and retain its valuable place in the community. These outcomes should justify adoption of a service plan.

Achieving both satisfaction and service quality requires a sustained, planned effort on the part of library management and staff to understand customer expectations, challenge themselves, and improve. They want to reduce the number of service failures and to offer services that delight customers and that are widely used. The service plan is central to doing this, and when that plan results in an award for quality, the library can market both the plan and the award among its stakeholders, customers, and funders.

Breakthrough organizations begin by creating listening posts to identify customer needs, then translate those needs back to the organization to design and deliver new and improved services.[11]

NOTES

1. Hardy R. Franklin, "Customer Service: The Heart of a Library," in *Libraries Change Lives: 1994 Campaign Book Supplement* (Chicago: American Library Assn., 1993), 8.

2. Susan Wehmeyer, Dorothy Auchter, and Arnold Hirshon, "Saying What We Will Do, and Doing What We Say: Implementing a Customer Service Plan," *Journal of Academic Librarianship* 22, no. 3 (May 1996): 173–80.

3. Peggy Wiehl, *William D. Ruckelshaus and the Environmental Protection Agency*, Case #9-375-083, Rev. 5/78 (Boston, Mass.: Harvard University Intercollegiate Case Clearing House, 1974), 5–6.

4. Jan Carlzon, *Moments of Truth* (New York: HarperCollins, 1987), 3.

5. Peter Hernon and Ellen Altman, *Service Quality in Academic Libraries* (Norwood, N.J.: Ablex, 1996), 51. See also Figure 6.2 for a partial list of dimensions for public libraries.

6. William H. Davidow and Bro Uttal, *Total Customer Service: The Ultimate Weapon* (New York: Harper Perennial, 1989), 23.

7. See Peter Hernon and Ellen Altman, *Assessing Service Quality: Satisfying the Expectations of Library Customers* (Chicago: American Library Assn., 1998), 79–99.

8. John R. Whitman, *Customer Focus at the Los Alamos National Laboratory Research Library: "Understand 'em and Give It to 'em!"* (Wellesley, Mass.: Surveytools Corp., 1999).

9. Hernon and Altman, *Assessing Service Quality*, chapter 7.

10. Whitman, *Customer Focus*. See also http://lib-www.lanl.gov/quality.

11. *Achieving Breakthrough Service in Libraries: A Nationwide Teleseminar Presented by the American Library Association* (Cambridge, Mass.: Kathleen Gilroy Assoc., 1994), 7.

6

Assessing and
Evaluating Satisfaction

*The ACSI [American Customer Satisfaction Index]
uses the only direct way to find out how satisfied or
dissatisfied people are—that is, to ask them.*[1]

A key step in the service plan is asking for feedback from customers and staff. This process is one of the defining aspects of the service quality and satisfaction relationship: giving customers a role to play in assessing how well the library delivers services and giving staff an opportunity to rate job satisfaction as well as to provide ideas about how to delight customers with the services provided. While the role of staff is key to delivering service quality and satisfaction, this chapter emphasizes customers. The feedback that customers provide is an exhilarating confirmation of all the hard work by management and staff alike to accommodate customer expectations. This chapter describes the actual process of soliciting and collecting such feedback and discusses how libraries can use the results of such an assessment in meaningful ways. Specifically, the chapter presents the distinction between assessment and evaluation; the general steps in conducting a survey; how to evaluate results; the importance of responding to customer comments and expectations; and several survey instruments, including a customer satisfaction questionnaire, an employee satisfaction questionnaire, a service improvement form, and a Web survey for public libraries.

(For specifics of conducting a survey, see *Assessing Service Quality* and *The Benevox Public Satisfaction System.*[2])

Assessment and Evaluation

The service plan presented in chapter 5 is based on a set of goals that, in turn, have measurable objectives that drive the implementation of the service plan. The results of the service plan are best demonstrated by the measurable consequences of the plan's goals and objectives. This measurable aspect suggests that it is possible to determine and quantify outcomes. Figure 6.1, "The Evaluation Wheel," illustrates the relationship among the tasks of collecting data, making sense of the data, and responding to the findings.

FIGURE 6.1
The Evaluation Wheel

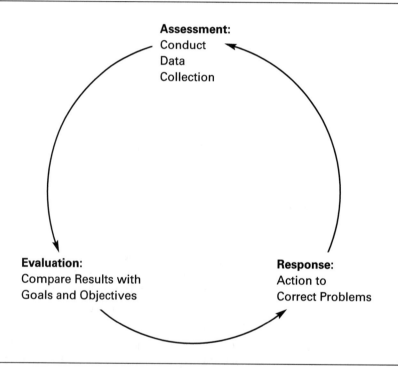

The *assessment process* is the task of collecting data. If the subject of the analysis is service quality, some of the required data may be collected through direct observation (e.g., of the length of time spent waiting in lines) or from transactional log analysis (i.e., the analysis of computer records of actual searching behavior). When customer satisfaction is the subject, a survey that captures reports made by the customers themselves is required. Assessment of customer satisfaction consists of five steps, which, taken collectively, are referred to as *conducting a survey*.

1. Designing and testing a questionnaire
2. Administering the questionnaire
3. Collecting the questionnaires
4. Entering the resulting data in a computer for analysis
5. Producing the analytical results in tables and graphs

The results of the assessment process, or survey, then become the basis on which management can evaluate the results, that is, consider the results in the light of service goals they are meant to measure. This process is called *evaluation*, and as the word implies, it involves applying value judgments. For example, the assessment data may indicate an average satisfaction score of 8.4 on a scale of 1 to 10, with 6 percent of respondents indicating a satisfaction score below 5. This is an example of an assessment finding, and by itself it provides no connection to the library's mission. The process of comparing this finding with the goal of achieving customer satisfaction necessarily involves a value judgment, which asks whether the 8.4 average and the 6 percent failure rate are an acceptable indication of achieving customer satisfaction. If the goal is to meet or exceed an average score of 8 and to limit failures to 5 percent or less, the evaluation concludes that the goal is only partially reached. Furthermore, the 6 percent failure rate indicates that there should be a review of the reasons for dissatisfaction among these respondents and a determination of what, if any, action is appropriate to prevent such failures in the future.

The distinction between assessment and evaluation is an important one, especially when dealing with a consultant hired to conduct a survey. The consultant may produce an excellent assessment report, presenting the findings in an orderly and understandable fashion, yet the task of evaluating the results typically lies beyond the capability of the consultant and remains the responsibility of those commissioning the study: the library director and members of the board or other policy body concerned with customer satisfaction. This is as it should be, since the library management is not only most familiar with the library's mission and goals but is in the best position to understand how the assessment results should be judged according to these guiding principles. Once the evaluation step is taken, the final remaining activity in this process is to initiate appropriate management action to correct probable causes of unacceptable results. This final activity represents the concluding step in the service plan.

Assessment: Conducting Surveys

The process presented in the evaluation wheel begins with collecting assessment data by conducting a survey either of service quality or satisfaction or both. The example used to illustrate this process involves the Customer Satisfaction Questionnaire for Public Libraries described in detail in the following sections.

Designing and Testing a Questionnaire

The Customer Satisfaction Questionnaire has been extensively used and repeatedly tested in public libraries. While it is presented here as a sample, it can be used with little modification. Clearly, the first modification required is to customize it by placing the library's name at the top of the questionnaire and making other appropriate changes to the form that are detailed in the following discussions. The library staff may be involved in reviewing the questionnaire and providing their comments on it. This exercise serves not only to get staff reaction to the questionnaire but also to alert staff to the coming assessment that customers will be asked to undertake and that will, in large measure, reflect how well the staff are performing. A further goal is to involve the staff in accepting and supporting the process.

Once the questionnaire is in a form suitable for distribution, it is advisable to test it by distributing it to thirty customers selected at random from the visiting population. A staff member might perhaps approach every tenth person entering the library and ask the customer kindly to complete and return the questionnaire before leaving the library. The staff member might say, for example, "Would you kindly help us by taking a moment to tell us how we're doing? Please complete our questionnaire and put it in that box before leaving today. Thank you very much." A box should be placed near the point of exit, and the customer should be offered a pencil to respond to the questions. This test will provide a preliminary sense of how well the questionnaire is working with the population and whether further modifications should be made prior to the full-scale survey.

Administering the Questionnaire

Once the questionnaire has been tested and modifications, if any, made, the next step is to print or photocopy as many copies of the questionnaire as are needed for the survey. This raises several questions:

Should all customers be surveyed, or should a sample be taken?

If a sample is taken, how many customers should be included, and how should they be selected?

When and how often should a survey be conducted?

If the survey is conducted once a year, what time of year should be selected?

A detailed consideration of these questions is beyond the scope of this book.[3] However the following general procedure is suggested as a standard format suitable for using the questionnaire. All customers might be given an opportunity to "vote," and they should be able to report what they think at any time. Therefore, the recommended approach is to take a sample, described as follows:

Place a stack of questionnaires throughout the year in locations in the library that visitors are most likely to frequent. Suggested locations include the reference and circulation desks and exit points. Provide pencils for completing the questionnaire, and place a box nearby for customers to return the forms without having to hand the form to an employee. This "suggestion box," or passive approach to hearing from customers, will work when customers are most motivated to send a message, which could happen at any time.

In addition, conduct an active survey for one or two weeks at least once every year or two. In such a survey, employees or volunteers (perhaps at a separate desk in the lobby that does not interfere with routine operations) ask customers to take a moment to respond to the questionnaire and return it prior to departing the library. Provide pencils so customers can respond on the spot. Since it may be difficult to ask every customer to respond, ask every tenth, fifteenth, or twentieth customer to respond. The goal is to select a reasonably representative sample so that responses may be received from the broadest range possible of the customer base and to collect at least 400 completed questionnaires, with few customers refusing to participate.

Conduct the survey daily over the one- to two-week period. The timing should reflect when the library is most likely to have the broadest range of customers visit the facility. Insert a copy of the questionnaire or print it in a library newsletter to coincide with the active survey.

David B. Pillemer suggests that customers' responses may differ, depending on whether they complete the questionnaire immediately following an experience at the library or respond the next day.[4] A more valid rating of overall satisfaction may result from waiting a day before responding to the questionnaire; however, other considerations argue for an immediate assessment. Memory of the details of one's experience may be lost when respondents are asked for a global, overall rating following a time lapse. For purposes of the proposed satisfaction survey, these details are at least as important as the validity of the overall satisfaction score. If a trade-off must be made, it is preferable to capture the details of possible sources of dissatisfaction in order to take remedial action and to accept a more conservative rating of overall satisfaction than to defer the rating of overall satisfaction at the cost of losing details that require attention. Two additional benefits of collecting the responses at the immediate conclusion of a visit are that the response rate is likely to be higher because waiting a day may result in misplaced questionnaires or a loss of interest in responding and that collecting the questionnaires at the door saves postage or another trip to return the questionnaire.

Some libraries experience seasonal variations, not only in the number of customers but also in those customers' principal uses for the library. For example, in a public library, school use may be high during the academic year but low during vacation periods. Careful attention must be paid to determining the best time to survey customers that will result in a reasonably representative sample. If customer activity changes dramatically between periods of light and heavy volume, conduct separate surveys, representing each type of period, and note the differences, if any. Customer experiences may be quite different depending on how busy the library is, and it is important to know how to improve service during both light and heavy periods.

Collecting the Questionnaires

Pay attention to which customers return the questionnaire. If a certain type of customer avoids responding, the resulting data will not be representative of the customer base. For example, perhaps very few mothers or fathers accompanying small children are taking the time to respond. This means that the survey will not include assessments by what could be an important segment of the library's customer base. In this case, the staff member handing out questionnaires might repeat the request to respond, as the library needs to include opinions from such customers.

It is not unheard of for some enthusiasts to "stuff the box" with favorable or unfavorable questionnaires. Naturally, this unfair practice creates a false picture and should be discouraged at the outset. In a similar vein, spirited children have been known to submit imaginative responses. These should be discreetly set aside, if possible, in order not to dilute the otherwise serious ratings that the library deserves. This is not to discredit earnest submissions by younger customers; the library should indeed be receptive to their perceptions and suggestions, not only because they are likely to be exposed to innovation in a variety of settings and can bring a fresh perspective to the library but also because they literally represent the future of the library.

Entering Results for Analysis

Once at least 400 questionnaires have been returned, the data are entered into the computer for analysis and interpretation. All responses to the open-response questions should be read carefully. Here, people will report what the library is doing right and what it could improve. By reading and understanding these open-ended responses, the statistics computed from number scales will be far more meaningful, and the survey far more valuable. Nonetheless, the staff should not overuse open-ended questions because such questions impose on the customers' time and can require considerable time for proper analysis.

Producing Analytical Results

Once the results are assembled, they may be posted in a central place accessible to everyone. This will let customers know that they have been heard. Because the recommended survey is ongoing, customers are invited to submit responses at any time. Nonparticipants in the active survey may be encouraged to add their opinions, especially if a stack of questionnaires is left adjacent to copies of the results. The results become the basis for conducting an evaluation of how well the library's mission and goals are being achieved.

Evaluation: Comparing Results with Goals

Once the assessment analysis is done, it is time to evaluate how well the library achieves its satisfaction goals. Notice that the assessment results alone are not sufficient to complete the evaluation. A raw score has little meaning without the process of interpreting it according to what that score represents. This is the role of evaluation, and it necessarily involves judgment. When the assessment results are analyzed, management should review them carefully against the mission's goals and objectives. The positive outcomes that can be documented will bolster confidence in executing the library's mission. The indication that some outcomes need attention will provide a focus on how to readdress expectations or take action to redress shortcomings in service delivery. Again, learning from these shortcomings improves service delivery, thereby, it is hoped, increasing customer overall satisfaction when next surveyed.

Response: Taking Action to Improve Outcomes

By responding to these perceived shortcomings, improvements are made. Whether indicated by customer comments or relatively low scores, these shortcomings demand attention. The survey results might be used to make a case to the funding source that additional resources may be needed to correct outcomes. In fact, the survey data provide documentation that might not otherwise exist to support a change, regardless of the ability to define the needed change. It can be instructive to keep a log of implemented changes (previously referred to as "change events") and to note whether satisfaction on these dimensions rises in the next survey. Whether the change in satisfaction is large or small, the net sum of actions to redress shortcomings should result in a higher overall satisfaction score on the next survey. There may, however, be new shortcomings addressed in each subsequent survey, and so the cycle repeats itself. Creating and measuring satisfaction is an ongoing process, not an end.

Sample Data-Collection Instruments

A survey questionnaire is a tool designed to ask the same set of questions of several people. This section presents the most important elements to include in a customer satisfaction questionnaire and provides sample questionnaires incorporating these elements (figures 6.2 and 6.3). The section also provides an example of a staff satisfaction questionnaire (figure 6.4) that may be used in conjunction with the customer satisfaction questionnaire. Finally, a service improvement report (figure 6.5) is described that can be used on an ongoing basis to collect immediate data on service incidents that may require attention.

The Customer Satisfaction Questionnaire

The customer satisfaction questionnaire, for either public or academic libraries, is one way to measure customer satisfaction (see figures 6.2 and 6.3). The questionnaire in figure 6.2, which is designed for use in a public library, may be modified for specialty uses.[5] This questionnaire gauges overall satisfaction and satisfaction with key service dimensions, and it provides customer feedback on issues that may need management attention. Once a survey using this questionnaire is completed, management may then wish to follow up with a focused study of a particular problem by employing a more specific survey questionnaire or conducting customer interviews or focus group interviews.

Upon its return each questionnaire should be numbered with a pen or pencil in the upper right corner of the first page. Starting with the number 1, each questionnaire has a unique number, which can be used to keep the questionnaires in order and facilitate locating the original copy of a particular questionnaire.

The title involves entering the name of the facility in place of "Library." The title is quite generic, but it is descriptive enough for the purposes of conducting such a survey. An address and telephone number may be added, but these are not necessary because a box in the library is used to collect completed questionnaires.

The opening words below the title serve as an introduction to the questionnaire. As shown in the public library example, this introduction is an opportunity to remind customers about what they should expect from the library. The respondent enters the date on which the questionnaire was completed. If the customer leaves out the date, the staff should enter it. A date should be associated with every questionnaire; otherwise, it will not be possible to associate particular assessments with a date or to compare responses over an extended period.

Following is a brief description of key items in figure 6.2. Variable names ascribed to the questions that offer a numeric response scale are indicated in italics. The order of the questions has been designed to capture the most important information first and to maximize the number of responses.

Overall, how satisfied are you with our library?

The first question captures a measure of *overall satisfaction*. Looking at this overall satisfaction score gives a sense of how service is being perceived. A score of 10 is, of course, exemplary. Satisfied customers will typically check in the 7 to 9 range, with a 7 indicating that they are moderately satisfied but that there is room for improvement. A score of 8 or above indicates very high satisfaction and is an appropriate target score for policy purposes. A score of 10 indicates that the customer is completely satisfied and that nothing can be improved. Because some people believe that nothing is perfect and there is always room for improvement (and therefore will not award a 10 on principle), a score of 9 indicates practical perfection. Scores that fall below a 7 merit close analysis to see what problems exist that are causing dissatisfaction. Any score below a 5 indicates that a customer is clearly dissatisfied; for the library staff to understand how the situation might be improved, they would need the respondent's name. It is possible that the customer was not aware of, or did not understand, the expectations that the library set. A simple clarification together with a suggestion for better meeting the customer's needs might be all that is needed.

FIGURE 6.2
Public Library Customer Satisfaction Questionnaire   Number: _____

We would like you to expect to find the resources you need in a comfortable, quiet, and pleasing environment. We would also like you to expect assistance from knowledgeable and courteous staff. Please take a moment to complete our questionnaire and tell us how we are doing. Thank you. *(Director's name)*

Today's date: _____

1. Overall, how satisfied are you with our library?

COMPLETELY DISSATISFIED									**COMPLETELY SATISFIED**
1	2	3	4	5	6	7	8	9	10

2. Please indicate whether we fall short of, exactly meet, or exceed your expectations:

FALL SHORT OF EXPECTATIONS			**EXACTLY MEET EXPECTATIONS**			**EXCEED EXPECTATIONS**
−3	−2	−1	0	+1	+2	+3

3. If you are not satisfied, please explain why not.

4. What do you like most about us?

5. What do you like least about us?

6. Please rate us on these items. (Skip the ones that are not applicable.)

	POOR									**EXCELLENT**
Adult books	1	2	3	4	5	6	7	8	9	10
Children's books	1	2	3	4	5	6	7	8	9	10
Periodicals	1	2	3	4	5	6	7	8	9	10
Reference materials	1	2	3	4	5	6	7	8	9	10
Films	1	2	3	4	5	6	7	8	9	10
Lectures	1	2	3	4	5	6	7	8	9	10
Educational programs	1	2	3	4	5	6	7	8	9	10
Audiotapes	1	2	3	4	5	6	7	8	9	10
Circulation desk	1	2	3	4	5	6	7	8	9	10
Internet access	1	2	3	4	5	6	7	8	9	10
Staff courtesy	1	2	3	4	5	6	7	8	9	10
Security	1	2	3	4	5	6	7	8	9	10
Washrooms	1	2	3	4	5	6	7	8	9	10
Convenient hours	1	2	3	4	5	6	7	8	9	10
Convenient location	1	2	3	4	5	6	7	8	9	10
Parking	1	2	3	4	5	6	7	8	9	10
Other (please specify) _____	1	2	3	4	5	6	7	8	9	10

Please see other side . . .

FIGURE 6.2
Public Library Customer Satisfaction Questionnaire (continued)

7. How important is this library to you?

NOT AT ALL
IMPORTANT

      EXTREMELY
      IMPORTANT

1   2   3   4   5   6   7   8   9   10

8. What is your primary use of this library? (Check all that apply.)

☐ Personal pleasure   ☐ Personal research   ☐ Work related

☐ School related   ☐ Children's use   ☐ Other (please specify): _____

9. How easy is it to find what you want?

NOT AT
ALL EASY

      EXTREMELY
      EASY

1   2   3   4   5   6   7   8   9   10

10. Are you a member of our library?   ☐ Yes   ☐ No   ☐ Do not know

11. How often do you come here?

☐ This is my first visit   ☐ Daily   ☐ Weekly   ☐ Monthly

☐ 4 times/year   ☐ 2 times/year   ☐ Once a year   ☐ Less than once a year

12. What is your age group?

☐ Under 13   ☐ 13–17   ☐ 18–24   ☐ 25–45   ☐ 46–64   ☐ 65 and up

13. If we could do one thing to improve, what would it be?

14. Please give us any other comments or suggestions you may have.

Optional

Your name: _____

City/town: _____

ZIP/postal code: _____

Telephone: _____

E-mail address: _____

Thank you very much.

FIGURE 6.3
Academic Library Customer Satisfaction Questionnaire   Number: _____

Please take a moment to complete our questionnaire and tell us how we are doing. Your candid responses wlll help us provide high-quality service. Thank you. *(Director's name)*

Today's date: _____

1. Overall, how satisfied are you with our library?

COMPLETELY DISSATISFIED									COMPLETELY SATISFIED
1	2	3	4	5	6	7	8	9	10

2. Please indicate whether we fall short of, exactly meet, or exceed your expectations:

FALL SHORT OF EXPECTATIONS			EXACTLY MEET EXPECTATIONS			EXCEED EXPECTATIONS
−3	−2	−1	0	+1	+2	+3

3. If you are not satisfied, please explain why not.

4. What do you like most about us?

5. What do you like least about us?

6. Please rate us on these items. (Skip the ones that are not applicable.)

	POOR									EXCELLENT
Monographs	1	2	3	4	5	6	7	8	9	10
Periodicals	1	2	3	4	5	6	7	8	9	10
Government publications	1	2	3	4	5	6	7	8	9	10
Maps	1	2	3	4	5	6	7	8	9	10
Reference materials	1	2	3	4	5	6	7	8	9	10
Other resources (please specify) _____	1	2	3	4	5	6	7	8	9	10
Staff courtesy	1	2	3	4	5	6	7	8	9	10
Location/retrieval assistance	1	2	3	4	5	6	7	8	9	10
Building temperature	1	2	3	4	5	6	7	8	9	10
Drinking fountains	1	2	3	4	5	6	7	8	9	10
Washrooms	1	2	3	4	5	6	7	8	9	10
Information literacy programs	1	2	3	4	5	6	7	8	9	10
Use of technology	1	2	3	4	5	6	7	8	9	10
Circulation services	1	2	3	4	5	6	7	8	9	10
Document delivery	1	2	3	4	5	6	7	8	9	10
Internet access	1	2	3	4	5	6	7	8	9	10
Interlibrary loans	1	2	3	4	5	6	7	8	9	10
Convenient hours	1	2	3	4	5	6	7	8	9	10
Personal security	1	2	3	4	5	6	7	8	9	10
Safety of my belongings	1	2	3	4	5	6	7	8	9	10
Other (please specify) _____	1	2	3	4	5	6	7	8	9	10

Please see other side . . .

7. How important is this library to you?

**NOT AT ALL
IMPORTANT**   **EXTREMELY
IMPORTANT**

    1   2   3   4   5   6   7   8   9   10

8. What is your primary use of this library? (Check all that apply.)

☐ Completion of classroom assignments   ☐ Teaching   ☐ Research/scholarly writing

☐ Personal pleasure   ☐ Consulting   ☐ Other (please specify) _____

9. How easy is it to find what you want?

**NOT AT
ALL EASY**   **EXTREMELY
EASY**

    1   2   3   4   5   6   7   8   9   10

10. How often do you come here?

☐ This is my first visit   ☐ Daily   ☐ Weekly   ☐ Monthly

☐ 4 times/year   ☐ 2 times/year   ☐ Once a year   ☐ Less than once a year

11. What best describes you?

☐ Undergraduate student   ☐ Graduate student   ☐ Staff   ☐ Other

☐ Faculty   ☐ Visiting faculty   ☐ Other visitor   (please specify) _____

12. What is your primary discipline?

☐ Behavioral sciences   ☐ Humanities   ☐ Law   ☐ Medical sciences

☐ Physical sciences   ☐ Social sciences   ☐ Education   ☐ Other (please specify) _____

13. If we could do one thing to improve, what would it be?

14. Please give us any other comments or suggestions you may have.

Optional

Your name: _____

Telephone: _____

E-mail address: _____

Thank you very much.

The placement of the overall satisfaction question as the first question is intentional. The purpose of the question is to capture what the respondent perceives to be his or her top-of-mind sense of satisfaction. This sense should not be colored or influenced by a preliminary consideration of any specific experiences, which are appropriately raised later in the questionnaire.

Please indicate whether we fall short of, exactly meet, or exceed your expectations.

The purpose of the second item is to get customers to report whether the library meets their service expectations. A score of 0 would mean that expectations were exactly met—nothing more, nothing less. Scores higher than 0 would indicate that service exceeds the customer's expectations. Scores below 0 indicate that the customer's expectations are not being met. This, in turn, indicates that a problem or misunderstanding should be identified and corrected. It could be, upon reflection, that the expectations being set are not completely or easily attainable.

Note that both the "satisfaction" and "expectations" scales are necessary. To the extent that satisfaction is based on expectations, the questionnaire will reveal how the overall satisfaction score compares with whether expectations were met. For example, if a customer rates the library a 10 on satisfaction (question 1) and a 0 on expectations (question 2), this means that the customer is totally satisfied, and that he or she expected this level of satisfaction according to the desired expectations. If a customer rates the library a 10 on satisfaction and above a 0 on expectations, that person feels that the library exceeds the expectations set. This may well mean that one or more employees did a truly outstanding job in assisting the customer in a way that was not expected. In other words, not only is satisfaction high but service is exceeding expectations to produce that satisfaction. The higher both numbers are, the more pleased the customer. Having only one of the scales provides only part of the picture; looking at these two questions together is key.

If expectations are set by clearly informing customers what they can expect from the library, and those expectations are consistently and exactly met over time, then it would not be surprising if most expectation scores were 0. Satisfaction scores and expectations scores correlate. It would be unusual to have a high score on one but a low score on the other; if so, it could indicate that there was an error in data entry or that the customer did not interpret the scale correctly. In such a case, the data can be corrected after the original questionnaire has been consulted, or the data entry for that response can be omitted.

If you are not satisfied, please explain why not.

The third item provides the customer with an opportunity to report specifically what is wrong. Since most people are likely to indicate a low satisfaction score if there is something specific that is causing them a problem, it is important to know what that problem is right away. This question is one that warrants attention and response with some urgency. Correcting a complaint from a single customer might improve the situation for many others who simply did not point it out in the current survey. Moreover, it is important to respond directly to customers who report dissatisfying experiences, if their identities are known, and to attempt to improve the situation for them as soon as possible. As Pillemer points out, "Developmental research supports the essential connection between talking about an event and remembering it later on."[6] Thus, asking customers to record (or talk about) their dissatisfying experience(s) may actually reinforce their memory as one of dissatisfaction, an outcome that is patently undesirable, even if justified. By taking immediate action to improve the situation for the customer, it is hoped that the situation will be reversed and remembered as a positive one with a satisfactory outcome.

What do you like most about us?

It is helpful to find out how customers perceive the strengths of the library. This question will help identify what is being done right, in the words of customers. Analyzing these responses could provide insights into service delivery. The wording that customers use could also help better define and describe services to others and could serve as anonymous testimonials for the library.

What do you like least about us?

This question is meant to elicit what customers think could be improved, even if it may not be causing them great dissatisfaction at the moment. In addition to the responses to the third item, on causes of dissatisfaction, responses to this question could be clustered and similar responses counted to measure the magnitude or extent of awareness of specific perceived problems. This provides a way to prioritize problems for action.

Please rate us on these items.

A dimension is a particular aspect of the facility or operation that people can measure individually and separately from their overall experience. As previously discussed, dimensions relate to expectations. The same ten-point scale applies. Notice that not all these dimensions may be appropriate for a particular facility. The selection of dimensions and their wording should be appropriate to the library being studied. Not all possible dimensions should be listed, only those that are the most important to measure. The customer will use the comments section to report missing issues of concern.

With all the attention in public libraries focusing on service responses (see chapter 4), some libraries might want to include dimensions that reflect the thirteen service response topics. For instance, libraries with literacy programs may want customers to rate such programs on a ten-point scale.

How important is this library to you?

This question attempts to place a numeric value on how important the public perceives the library to be. Importance is useful for several reasons: It provides a way to quantify how important the library is to its customers as reported by the customers themselves. It also offers a basis on which to compare other survey findings and their satisfaction scores. Greater attention may be paid to responses from customers who report higher importance scores. It is also useful to understand why some customers may not perceive the library as highly important.

Instead of or in addition to the question about importance, library evaluators might query customers about the value of library services—an estimation of "the direct return on annual taxpayer investment in their organizations."[7]

What is your primary use of the library?

This question is key to segmenting the customer base. Customers who use the facility in different ways may have different expectations of the facility; therefore, they may report different overall satisfaction scores. This question will also reveal how people who use the facility for different purposes respond to the other survey questions. Depending on the mission of the library, responses to this question can be appropriately reworded. (See figure 6.3 as an example.)

How easy is it to find what you want?

Cross-tabulating these ease-of-use responses with the primary use of the facility will point to areas that may need attention (see chapter 8).

Are you a member of our library?

For a public library, membership represents another way to segment the customer base. The process of applying for membership allows the opportunity to set clear expectations—putting the library in control of determining the basis for satisfaction—and to educate the customers on how best to use the library. Also, this question will alert nonmember visitors to the possibility of membership. Academic and special libraries may want to substitute "Do you have a library card?"

How often do you come here?

The choice of categories for this question can be modified. Frequency of visits is an indicator of library importance or value.

What is your age group?

Age is yet another way to segment the customer base. Although the specific age categories can be modified, it makes sense to standardize them when conducting year-after-year surveys so that results can easily be compared across surveys. Because this question is oriented primarily to public libraries, other library types would probably omit it.

Final questions.

The final questions are self-explanatory. The identifying information should be optional to preserve the anonymity of a customer with a complaint. Respondents who provide low scores and include their names should be contacted to thank them for their comments, find out specifically what their problems were, and offer to correct them. Library management concerned that customers might be offended or concerned about invasion of privacy by an effort to solicit their names and ways to contact them should forgo asking respondents to identify themselves. If such information is essential, the introduction to the survey should attempt to dissuade such concerns.

The city/town information provides an indication of whether the visitor is local. Some libraries want to know specifically where their customers come from. In such a case, an additional question prior to this one can be included that asks, for example, "What is your home ZIP code?" Where customers may be seasonal, two questions may be necessary, such as "What is the ZIP code of your permanent address?" followed by "If you are a seasonal resident in this area, what is the ZIP code of your local address?" In academic libraries, individual anonymity can be preserved while still requesting the names of a department or administrative area, if such information would be useful to the survey. The number of respondents who provide an e-mail address will provide an indication of Internet use.

The academic library questionnaire is derived from the one for the public library. Although it is substantially the same as figure 6.2, figure 6.3 lists dimensions, usage, and customer profile questions that are pertinent to academic libraries.

The Staff Satisfaction Questionnaire

Figure 6.4 presents a Staff Satisfaction Questionnaire that makes it easy for employees to report job satisfaction and provide ideas on how to improve customer satisfaction.[8] Since there may be a general correlation between staff and customer satisfaction, average overall satisfaction scores for staff could be compared with average overall customer scores over time.

Because employees are dependent on the library for income, they may not be as forthcoming as customers in reporting dissatisfaction and causes of dissatisfaction. This suggests potential validity problems with an employee satisfaction questionnaire. The degree to which employees feel comfortable sharing their assessments can reflect how secure they feel in doing so. Therefore, employee responses should be treated carefully to support the spirit of constructive dialogue. Especially important in this regard is not to use the results of an employee satisfaction assessment as the basis for adverse action against an employee; rather, the questionnaire should be used as an opportunity to report what he or she thinks could be improved in a way that will benefit not only employees but also customers.

FIGURE 6.4
Staff Satisfaction Questionnaire

When you joined us you probably had expectations of your job that included the type of work you would be doing, the working environment, your colleagues, and other dimensions of your employment. This questionnaire will help us understand how you assess your job situation at this time, and give you the opportunity to tell us what you think about your job. Please respond candidly. Your assessment is very important. Thank you.

Today's date: _____

1. Overall, how satisfied are you in your current position?

COMPLETELY DISSATISFIED									**COMPLETELY SATISFIED**
1	2	3	4	5	6	7	8	9	10

2. Please indicate whether your job falls short of, exactly meets, or exceeds your expectations:

FALLS SHORT OF EXPECTATIONS			**EXACTLY MEETS EXPECTATIONS**			**EXCEEDS EXPECTATIONS**
−3	−2	−1	0	+1	+2	+3

3. If you are not satisfied, please explain why not.

4. What do you like most about working here?

5. What do you like least about working here?

6. Please rate your working experience on these items. (Skip the ones that are not applicable.)

	POOR									**EXCELLENT**
Overall working conditions	1	2	3	4	5	6	7	8	9	10
My personal working environment	1	2	3	4	5	6	7	8	9	10
Helpfulness/support from other employees	1	2	3	4	5	6	7	8	9	10
Helpfulness/support from my supervisor	1	2	3	4	5	6	7	8	9	10
Authority to achieve results for our users	1	2	3	4	5	6	7	8	9	10
Feeling of reward from helping our users	1	2	3	4	5	6	7	8	9	10
Receiving recognition for my performance	1	2	3	4	5	6	7	8	9	10
Adequate training to perform my job	1	2	3	4	5	6	7	8	9	10
Working hours	1	2	3	4	5	6	7	8	9	10
Adequate compensation	1	2	3	4	5	6	7	8	9	10
Benefits program	1	2	3	4	5	6	7	8	9	10
Adequate vacation policy	1	2	3	4	5	6	7	8	9	10
Ability to take time off when needed	1	2	3	4	5	6	7	8	9	10
Other (please specify) _____	1	2	3	4	5	6	7	8	9	10

Please see other side . . .

FIGURE 6.4
Staff Satisfaction Questionnaire (continued)

7. Please indicate your staff status here.

☐ Full-time employee ☐ Part-time employee ☐ Full-time volunteer

☐ Part-time volunteer ☐ Other (please specify) _____

8. How would you like to see your job or working environment most improved?

9. Do you have any specific ideas about how we can improve customer satisfaction?

10. Please give us any other comments or suggestions you may have.

Optional

Your name: _____

Thank you very much.

The employee satisfaction questions are generally self-explanatory, and some are duplicates of or parallel to those appearing on the customer satisfaction questionnaire. As with the customer questionnaire, the dimensions on the employee questionnaire should be selected based on the actual conditions at the library.[9]

The Service Improvement Report

In addition to the satisfaction questionnaires, both customers and employees should have at their disposal a means to report at any time any problem or suggestion regarding service delivery. Maintain a stock of service improvement report forms at the reference and circulation desks and at other points of service delivery in the library. The form, presented in figure 6.5, is adapted from the Opportunity for Process Improvement (OPPI) form used by the Research Library at the Los Alamos National Laboratory. There, OPPI forms are given to every staff member and are available to customers at the reference desk. An OPPI can be completed any time a staff member interacts with a customer. The OPPI form captures the customer's name, group, and telephone number; any appropriate comments or a description of the interaction; and the resolution of the matter. If the customer does not initiate a response, the staff member will, thus capturing the lessons learned from the interaction. OPPIs record both suggestions and, not infrequently, compliments; both are welcome. When an OPPI is registered by the customer, he or she always receives an acknowledgment, signifying that the communication is in process.[10]

The difference between this reporting format and that of a typical comment card or suggestion box is that library staff should be instructed to use the service report forms *every* time they identify an opportunity to improve the service delivery process. This is not a passive approach that is contingent on the customer to take a reporting initiative. When a service improvement report is completed, it should be delivered to the director for attention or to someone assigned to this role. This is a way for the library to recognize specific lapses in service delivery, possible service failures, suggestions for improvement, or other issues requiring attention throughout the year, regardless of the timing of a satisfaction survey. How the library acts upon these reports may have an impact on the findings of subsequent satisfaction studies. Certainly, service improvement reports will play an important role in providing the needed feedback loops among customers, employees, and management.

Workshop Evaluation Questionnaire

Figure 6.6 is an evaluation form for a workshop or course offered by either an academic or public library. Statements for question 6 could be adapted to address other issues. This form combines open-ended questions for which brief responses are desired and the ten-point numeric scale. For any responses of less than a 7, the staff should pay close attention to the open-ended questions. If the same program or course will be offered repeatedly, evaluators could monitor and compare responses.

FIGURE 6.5
Service Improvement Report

To Customers and Staff: Please use this form either to report outstanding service by our staff or to suggest an opportunity for improvement. This can include service delivery, availability of specific items or resources, improvements in the facility, and any other suggestions you might have for improvement. Your report will be sent to the Director's office. Thank you.

Date/time of service report: _____

Are you offering a:

a. ☐ Compliment

b. ☐ Suggestion for improvement

c. ☐ Other (please specify) _____

What department or service area are you commenting on?

Your comments:

Optional

Name: _____

Telephone: _____

E-mail: _____

For Administration
Action Taken:

Was that action satisfactory to resolve the incident?
   a. ____ Yes   b. ____ No   c. ____ In progress
Comment:

Modified from the Opportunity for Process Improvement form, the Los Alamos National Laboratory Library.

FIGURE 6.6
Workshop Evaluation Questionnaire

Thank you for attending this workshop. It is our hope that what you have learned is valuable to you. To let us know how we did and how we can improve, please complete and return this questionnaire before leaving.

Workshop date: _____

1. Overall, how satisfied were you with this workshop?

COMPLETELY DISSATISFIED									COMPLETELY SATISFIED
1	2	3	4	5	6	7	8	9	10

2. Please indicate whether we fell short of, exactly met, or exceeded your expectations:

FELL SHORT OF EXPECTATIONS			EXACTLY MET EXPECTATIONS			EXCEEDED EXPECTATIONS
−3	−2	−1	0	+1	+2	+3

3. If you were not satisfied, please explain why not.

4. What did you like most about the workshop?

5. What did you like least about the workshop?

6. Please rate the workshop on these items. (Skip the ones that are not applicable.)

	POOR									EXCELLENT
Objectives of the workshop	1	2	3	4	5	6	7	8	9	10
Value of the material to you	1	2	3	4	5	6	7	8	9	10
Sustained level of interest	1	2	3	4	5	6	7	8	9	10
Organization of presentation	1	2	3	4	5	6	7	8	9	10
Audio/visual use	1	2	3	4	5	6	7	8	9	10
Use of computer technology	1	2	3	4	5	6	7	8	9	10
Length of workshop	1	2	3	4	5	6	7	8	9	10
Cleanliness of the facility	1	2	3	4	5	6	7	8	9	10
Lighting in the facility	1	2	3	4	5	6	7	8	9	10
Room comfort	1	2	3	4	5	6	7	8	9	10
Other (please specify) _____	1	2	3	4	5	6	7	8	9	10

Please see other side . . .

FIGURE 6.6
Workshop Evaluation Questionnaire (continued)

7. Would you recommend this workshop to others?

   ☐ Yes   ☐ No   ☐ Not sure

8. What additional topics would you like added to the workshop?

9. How did you hear about this workshop?

   a. ☐ Direct mailing   d. ☐ Internet (please specify where) _____

   b. ☐ Colleague   e. ☐ Newsletter

   c. ☐ E-mail notice   f. ☐ Other (please specify) _____

10. Please give us any other comments or suggestinos you may have.

Thank you very much.

Summary

Satisfaction questionnaires can be—and are—designed in a multitude of ways. Most, if not all, libraries certainly have staff capable of designing satisfaction questionnaires. It can be helpful in designing any survey to have an example questionnaire that has proven useful and that can serve as a starting point for a customized questionnaire. Two such survey instruments are a customer satisfaction questionnaire and a staff satisfaction questionnaire. Additionally, a service improvement report form can serve as an ongoing means for customers or staff to report incidents that require attention.

These specific feedback forms are central to executing the library's service plan. They are tools to make it easy for customers and staff to report satisfaction and their particular concerns, and they can be used as is, with very little modification. The resulting assessment data will provide the basis for an evaluation of how well the library is achieving its mission and service goals. The evaluation, together with a focus on service quality, can result in recommended action to correct service problems and can even point to the need to revise the mission or the service goals.

One of the most gratifying ways of making clear how important your employees are is to create opportunities for your customers to praise them. You can do this with customer surveys or reaction cards, particularly ones that request the name of particularly outstanding employees and examples of great service performances. Such surveys and comment cards have a remarkably tonic effect on employee morale: they show employees that they affect real people, that they do not labor in unappreciated anonymity.[11]

NOTES

1. University of Michigan Business School, National Quality Research Center, *The American Customer Satisfaction Index: Methodological Report* (Milwaukee: American Society for Quality, 1998), 15.

2. See Peter Hernon and Ellen Altman, *Assessing Service Quality: Satisfying the Expectations of Library Customers* (Chicago: American Library Assn., 1998), chapters 7 and 10. See also John R. Whitman, *The Benevox Public Satisfaction System* (Wellesley, Mass.: Surveytools Corp., 1998).

3. Hernon and Altman, *Assessing Service Quality*, chapters 7 and 10; Whitman, *The Benevox Public Satisfaction System*.

4. David B. Pillemer, *Momentous Events, Vivid Memories: How Unforgettable Moments Help Us Understand the Meaning of Our Lives* (Cambridge, Mass.: Harvard University Press, 1998), 60.

5. Whitman, *The Benevox Public Satisfaction System.*

6. Pillemer, *Momentous Events, Vivid Memories,* 127.

7. Glen E. Holt, Donald Elliott, and Amonia Moore, "Placing a Value on Public Library Service," *Public Libraries* 38, no. 2 (March/April 1999): 98–108.

8. Whitman, *The Benevox Public Satisfaction System.*

9. The questionnaires in figure 6.2, 6.3, 6.4, and 6.6 are used with permission of Surveytools Corp. The company allows use of these questionnaires on an as-is basis or with slight modifications, provided that the questionnaires are used by libraries that purchase this book, that the questionnaires will not be used to generate any income, and that Surveytools' copyright is protected. If any of the questionnaires are used, the following notice must be included on the questionnaire: Form Copyright © by Surveytools Corporation. ALL RIGHTS RESERVED.

10. See John R. Whitman, *Customer Focus at the Los Alamos National Laboratory Research Library: "Understand 'em and Give It to 'em!"* (Wellesley, Mass.: Surveytools Corp., 1999).

11. Bill Fromm and Len Schlesinger, *The Real Heroes of Business: And Not a CEO among Them* (New York: Doubleday, 1993), 87.

7 Using Computer Technology to Conduct Surveys

Use of the World Wide Web to conduct surveys provides enormous opportunities as well as challenges.[1]

There is no question that the personal computer of today can play a useful role in managing customer relationships in a broad range of organizations, including libraries. A sample of applications includes, for instance:

- being able to produce a list of borrowers
- tracking the use of the library's services and some electronic products
- preparing letters, newsletters, questionnaires, and other communications for customers
- maintaining an inventory of the library holdings
- using the Internet to extend access to the library to customers beyond the physical building
- using the Internet to allow customers to view the online public access catalog
- using the Internet to allow customers to reserve books
- using the Internet to conduct customer surveys
- storing results of surveys

- analyzing and presenting graphical reports on survey results
- using e-mail to send pertinent information to customers and to answer questions submitted by e-mail

This chapter does not explore all of these applications; instead, it focuses on using personal computers to conduct surveys and looks at questionnaire design, data entry, analysis, and reporting. The chapter discusses several options for using computer technology; explores how to use the Internet as a resource for conducting surveys, specifically on the World Wide Web and by e-mail; and identifies several pros and cons to consider in doing so. As technology is making it easier and faster to conduct and analyze surveys, the corresponding growth in the use of surveys may result in a general public backlash against responding to them. This is an important reason to use surveys judiciously and to take special care to ensure that their purpose and design invite participation.

Survey Software

The service plan described in chapters 5 and 6 clearly involves the collection and processing of a large amount of data in the course of conducting either a service quality or satisfaction survey. Several computer software packages that can help manage this process are available. Generally, there are two approaches to using a personal computer for conducting surveys: the assembled approach and the integrated approach.

Assembled Approach

The assembled approach is best described as using different software applications or packages for the various steps in conducting a survey. For example, a word-processing package may be used to design and print a questionnaire form and a separate database package to store survey results. Alternatively, a spreadsheet package can store and analyze results. Finally, depending on the graphical capabilities of the analysis package, a specialized graphics package or the graphical utilities in a spreadsheet package can be used to present the results of data analysis in a graphical format. Several software firms, such as Corel, Lotus, and Microsoft, offer so-called office suites that include a set of word-processing, database, and spreadsheet applications that are general purpose applications but that can easily be used in survey research. Additionally, SPSS, formerly the Statistical Package for the Social Sciences, offers several stand-alone modules especially designed for questionnaire design, data entry, statistical analysis, and graphical presentation.[2] These applications can be used separately or in conjunction with each other.

Users of the assembled approach need to be somewhat proficient in the various software applications and confident in their ability to transfer results from one package to another. A benefit of this approach is that there is a great deal of flexibility in designing the questionnaire, entering data into the computer, analyzing the data, and formatting reports. It is not unusual to select one package specifically to enter the data and then to use its file-exporting option to transfer the data to another package for statistical analysis.

Integrated Approach

The integrated approach is best described as combining several or all of the survey steps into a single software package, typically presented as a "complete solution" for survey needs. Several such more or less integrated packages are available in the market.[3] With integrated software, users will be able to design a questionnaire, store the resulting data, analyze the data, and produce attractive reports, all within the same package.

The ease of use and options afforded by such packages, particularly SurveyPro, make them well suited for many uncomplicated survey uses, including service quality and customer satisfaction surveys. Users who want to conduct sophisticated statistical analyses that may not be included in such packages can easily export the data for analysis in a larger, more complex statistical package, such as SPSS.

Data Entry

A major consideration in the use of survey software is how response data are entered into the computer for analysis, a process generally called *data entry* or, to use an older term, *keypunching*. Some integrated packages offer an option that enables the respondent to view the questionnaire on a computer and to respond by entering data directly into the computer. A variation on this technique is to involve a researcher in entering the data during a telephone interview, computer-assisted telephone interview (CATI), face-to-face interview, or computer-assisted personal interview (CAPI) with the respondent. The chief advantage of these options is that the data are entered directly into the computer by the respondent (or a researcher), eliminating the need to produce a paper version of the questionnaire that would require subsequent manual data entry, which could result in data entry errors. Furthermore, many software applications for this purpose include the ability to check automatically that the data entered are appropriate to the question being posed, thus reducing the likelihood of entering erroneous responses.

When paper questionnaires are preferred or must be used, one still has options for data entry. Several companies, notably Scantron Corporation and National Computer Systems, Inc., offer products and services to create questionnaires in machine-readable formats.[4] The completed questionnaires can be read by special scanners that convert the marks on the questionnaire into data stored in the computer. Alternatively, Principia Products, Inc., sells software that scans a questionnaire created in a standard word-processing format and programs the scanner to recognize and convert the responses into data stored in the computer.[5] Both of these options require the use of a special or general-purpose scanner. The two types of scanning possibilities are optical mark readers (OMR) and optical character readers (OCR). OMRs read only marks (blackened segments on the questionnaire), which means that all questions must be limited-choice. OCRs attempt to read written characters placed in delineated blocks on the questionnaire. While scanners can make the data entry process easier, particularly when large numbers of questionnaires must be processed, they are also subject to error, principally caused by extraneous marks, folds, or tears on the form.

The most widely practiced means of data entry remains the manual approach, whereby someone enters the data into the computer by hand through the keyboard. This is the recommended approach for entering the data from the survey questionnaires presented in chapter 6. Statistical and database software programs offer one or more data entry formats that are more or less adequate for the task. A typical format is the familiar spreadsheet format, where each row (or line) corresponds to a different questionnaire record, and each column represents a different question or variable. Because of the possibility of data entry error, some packages offer an option to check for error by requiring that the data for each questionnaire be entered twice in succession. Some statistical programs offering graphical reports recommend that numeric data be displayed in a scatterplot format to display outlying data points that might indicate erroneous values and that cross tabulations of variables be conducted. The purpose is to identify erroneous combinations of data, such as the number of pregnant males, or, in the case of a satisfaction survey, incidents in which a high "overall satisfaction" score might appear in combination with a very low "expectations" score. The process of checking for and correcting such errors is often called *data cleaning*.

To test the quality of data entry, at least thirty cases should be selected at random and manually checked against the original questionnaires. Where errors are discovered, additional errors may have been made in the process of data entry. This may require that all questionnaires be similarly proofread against the entered data.

Data Analysis

For the purposes of the surveys presented in this book, a simple statistical package should be sufficient for data analysis. It is possible to employ a spreadsheet package to do the data analysis, as most offer the basic descriptive statistics necessary for analysis; however, this approach may prove more cumbersome than using a program especially designed for statistical data entry and analysis. If the library expects to conduct a variety of relatively simple surveys beyond those suggested in this book, it may be sensible to invest in an integrated package such as SurveyPro. SurveyPro is simple and easy to learn but offers limited, though adequate, statistical analysis. In any case, files can be exported to more-powerful analysis packages.

If the library intends to limit its surveys to the satisfaction surveys described in this book, it would be a short and simple process to produce the questionnaires using a word processor and then use Abstat to produce reports.[6] Abstat produces all the recommended statistics, and its character-based charts showing counts are all that are needed. If the library plans to conduct additional surveys involving the use of new questions, SurveyPro would be an excellent choice. If the library has a need for industrial-strength statistical analysis beyond the requirements to conduct the surveys suggested in this book (and if the staff are trained in the use of statistics), SPSS may be the preferred choice. This is a stand-alone package and does not include a built-in questionnaire design capability. The company does, however, offer various additional options, including one for questionnaire design.

Firms specialize in providing data entry services for survey research. Clients may contract with them to enter data from the questionnaires into a computer format appropriate for whichever software package will be used for the analysis. Some of these firms can also provide data analysis according to specifications set by the client. Such services may be found in the *Yellow Pages* under the "market research and analysis" section. While their use can alleviate the burden of data entry and analysis, it can also greatly increase the cost of the project.

Because of the growing use of the Internet as a means to collect data, many integrated survey packages are extending their capabilities to include Web and e-mail surveys. Comparing the features and options among these packages will reveal their strengths and weaknesses.

Web Surveys

A Web survey is one in which a questionnaire is placed at a Web site and respondents can complete the questionnaire form using their Web browser on the Internet. The questionnaire itself is simply a form that presents questions followed by choices to select or fields for data entry. If questionnaire writers are adept at creating Web forms using HTML, CGI, and perhaps Perl and Java, they can create a questionnaire on the Web and capture respondent data for storage in a file that can then be analyzed using statistical software. A number of companies, including Infopoll and WebSurveyor, provide specialized Web survey software and services, making it unnecessary to learn a specialized Web language.[7] The typical configuration of such software, using Infopoll as an example, is as follows.

A "client" software program will allow one to create a survey questionnaire. (A survey questionnaire designer can be downloaded from Infopoll for free.) The writer uses this program on a local computer working offline, that is, without being logged on to the Internet. The software typically involves dragging and dropping the various question types from a library of standard types to a form that is constructed in a workspace on the screen. The writer can determine the wording of the questions, appropriate response categories, and order in which the questions appear on the form. When finished, the questionnaire is saved to a file on the local computer. The writer can then choose to "publish" the questionnaire to another machine acting as a server on which special software further processes the questionnaire form and makes it active on the Web.

The server software program takes the questionnaire, presents it on the Internet, collects the data entered by respondents, stores the data, analyzes the data, and presents a report based on the analysis. This server software can either be on a local machine, on a server machine operated by a library, or on a remote server operated by the vendor company (as it is with Infopoll). In this latter case, the vendor company allows the user to conduct surveys using questionnaires designed by the user with a client software program; however, the resulting data are collected, stored, and analyzed on the vendor server, for which the user pays a fee. The fee is substantially less than purchasing a license to operate the server software on the user's local machine or server, and a staff member does not have to be responsible for administering the server software. In the case of both Infopoll and WebSurveyor, surveys may be purchased one at a time as needed, thus keeping costs as low as possible. The decision whether to purchase a server license or to pay a fee each time the user needs to conduct a survey is usually a matter of determining how many surveys will be conducted over a period of time and selecting the lowest cost option, bearing in mind the need for a server software administrator.

The questionnaire form itself can be located on the library's Web site or on the Web site of the company whose software is being used. (In either case, the HTML code within the form must contain an instruction that sends the resulting data to the server software for collection and analysis.) Once the questionnaire is made available to respondents and they begin to enter their responses, the data are sent to the server for storage, analysis, and presentation in the form of preformatted reports. These reports can be prepared following completion of the survey or in real time while the survey is in progress. The reports are accessible by browser, but access is typically protected by a password determined by the survey administrator.

Web surveys are an excellent way to collect survey data, provided that certain conditions are considered. Once it is on the Internet, the questionnaire is immediately accessible to respondents who have access to the Internet. They may need a password to complete the survey. The data entered by the respondent go directly into storage; and, as mentioned, the results of the survey can be tabulated and reported in real time, even as people are responding to it. A separate password may be required to allow viewing of the results.

Despite these features, there are several conditions and shortcomings that should be considered:

1. There is no simple and reliable way to make sure that the same person does not respond to the questionnaire more than once. Of course, the same problem arises in the use of paper questionnaires, but the practice may be more difficult to detect when the data are entered remotely via computer.

2. The appearance of the questionnaire is subject to constraints determined by the size, shape, and resolution of the respondent's computer screen, and this may vary among different computers. Furthermore, the appearance on a computer screen will almost always vary from that of a paper version of the same questionnaire.

3. A respondent cannot enter marginal comments or responses that could be important. In a Web questionnaire, the respondent is limited to selecting the offered responses or entering a response in a field for open-ended comments. On a paper questionnaire, the respondent can write comments anywhere on the form.

4. If a question type involves rating a long list of dimensions using the same scale, the scale labels, offered at the top of the list, can scroll off the screen, depending on the size of the respondent's screen.

Thus, the respondent must memorize the values for the scale, which can lead to response error.

5. Questions involving ranking typically require special Javascript coding, which can work differently in different browsers (and may not work at all in some). This can affect the reliability of the questionnaire.

6. Questions that request open-ended responses must set a limit on the length of the response. This limit, if too short, will prevent respondents from providing a complete response.

7. Error can be introduced when the respondent's mouse is not functioning properly. Mice are frequently affected by lint and other small debris in a manner sometimes referred to as "spastic mouse syndrome" manifested by a cursor that unexpectedly jumps around the screen. This can occur when a respondent selects a response to a question and the cursor jumps to a different area on the screen, resulting in the inadvertent selection of an unintended response. This phenomenon is not always caught by the respondent at the time, thus creating an undetected response error, reducing the quality of the survey results. (This problem appears to be exacerbated by the use of drop-down response type lists, which typically disappear once the mouse button is clicked.)

8. When survey data are collected on the vendor company's server, confidentiality is not within the library's control. In any case, confidentiality is very difficult to protect completely because respondents can technically be identified through their Internet Service Providers (ISPs) and by other means that electronically track communications on the Internet.

9. While it is simple to create a questionnaire form using most software available for this purpose, the writer is mostly limited to the question-and-response formats offered by the software, thus limiting the ability to customize the appearance of a questionnaire.

10. The analytical and reporting options offered by many Web survey software vendors are often limited to meeting basic needs and may not be adequate for more-sophisticated analysis.

11. Setting up and deleting a questionnaire might involve action by an administrator, either in the library or at the vendor's company, thus placing an additional step and level of human intervention in the process of executing a survey.

12. Perhaps most obviously, the questionnaire on the Web will only be available to those who have access to the Internet. This means that the population being surveyed will, by definition, be limited to Internet users.

If librarians wish to conduct both a Web survey and a corresponding paper questionnaire, they should be mindful of how these different forms can affect responses in different ways, thus affecting the quality of the survey. In connection with this final concern, it should be noted that the library's Web site in general, and any use of Web surveys in particular, should take into consideration the needs of disabled Internet users. This is an area of interest to the Center for Applied Special Technology (http://www.cast.org), which provides a free analysis of Web pages for their accessibility to people with disabilities.

In view of these considerations, it makes most sense to conduct a survey on the Web when the entire sample to be surveyed is already using the Web and no one will be disadvantaged by the survey availability or format on the Web. It may also make sense to post a questionnaire on the Web when undertaking a survey that also uses other modes of response, such as paper-and-pencil or e-mail. This will give respondents the option to choose the mode of response most convenient to them. Again, note that multiple formats for response may affect the reliability of the survey. To test such a possibility would require coding each response according to the mode used and then comparing responses by mode to detect any significant difference that might be attributable to the particular mode used.

In addition to providing customer and staff satisfaction questionnaires as described in chapter 5, Surveytools Corporation maintains a standard customer satisfaction questionnaire on the Internet that is meant specifically for public libraries but that can easily be modified for other types of libraries. This questionnaire (http://www.surveytools.com/library), which was designed using the Infopoll software, can be completed by anyone with browser access to the Internet. The questionnaire is virtually identical to the sample questionnaire for public libraries presented in figure 6.2.

Responses are collected, reviewed, and sent by Surveytools to the library identified and rated by the respondent. One way for a library to use this questionnaire immediately is by bookmarking the site on one or more Internet-connected computers in the library so that customers can complete the questionnaire while visiting the library. For a fee, the questionnaire can be modified or customized for a particular library and posted at that library's Web site, where it would be available for response only by the population served by that library. A Web survey such as this, however, does not replace the need for a more inclusive survey project that will reach customers who do not have access to the Internet.

E-Mail Surveys

An e-mail survey is one in which a questionnaire is sent by e-mail to respondents. There are, at present, two general ways in which e-mail surveys are conducted: manual and professional. *Manual e-mail* refers to the procedure by which one prepares the survey questionnaire within the body of an outgoing e-mail and instructs respondents to answer by one of the following methods:

  using the reply feature, so that their responses are returned to the sender by e-mail

  going to a survey questionnaire on the Web, which respondents may then complete without responding directly to the e-mail printing out the questionnaire contained in the e-mail, completing it by hand, and returning it to the sender (or another destination) by mail or by fax

arranging for a telephone interview to respond to the questions

An e-mail survey does not necessarily involve attaching a questionnaire file, such as a questionnaire formatted in a word processor. Of course, attaching a file is always an option, but that could require the respondent to use other software, such as a word processor, to open the attached file. The recommended approach includes the questionnaire within the body of the e-mail message, so no attachment is necessary.

Professional e-mail refers to the use of a specialty survey package that offers a self-contained way to create a questionnaire, transmit it by e-mail, and collect responses by e-mail. This package is an example of the "integrated" software approach described earlier in this chapter.[8]

The use of e-mail surveys raises several concerns:

1. E-mail can be sent only to those whose e-mail addresses are known. Because people can change their e-mail addresses at any time, a sample may not be accurate at the time the survey is executed. Unless the e-mail questionnaire is returned to the sender, one may not know for certain whether it was received by the intended recipients.

2. Often, a firewall or other blocking mechanism may prevent an e-mail questionnaire from reaching an intended recipient. There is little that can be done about this because firewall maintenance is often strictly controlled.

3. Individuals in the sample may not wish to receive surveys by e-mail. They may regard such a message as an undesirable, commercial mass-mailing and may delete the message before opening it or may simply ignore it.

4. As in Web surveys, the survey and, in particular, the response data are not private, so confidentiality cannot be assured. This is especially problematic when e-mail is sent to a respondent's address on his or her employer's server and it is the policy in that business to monitor employee e-mail.

5. Some respondents may change the response format, which will thwart the software's ability to process their response correctly and will result in errors.

Nevertheless, e-mail questionnaires have a number of advantages:

Respondents need only select *reply* to respond to the questionnaire, which is transmitted directly back to the sender. Thus, e-mail questionnaires can allow very fast response times.

The questionnaire can be printed out and faxed or mailed back, but this involves additional cost.

Respondents can write as much as they like because there is virtually no limit to the length of a response, as there is with Web surveys.

Respondents do not need to open a browser or go somewhere else on the Web to respond, eliminating this additional step.

E-mail surveys do not require the use of specialty "client" and "server" software programs, nor do they require a special administrator, as do some Web survey packages.

The cost of conducting the survey is minimal. No postage is required, and any follow-up is low in cost.

Summary

Libraries have a number of choices of how to use computers in their operations and of which software packages are best suited to their needs. The market offers a range of solutions, which can include integrated or stand-alone functionality. No single choice is suitable for all libraries, and upgrades to existing solutions as well as new entries to the market are constantly being offered. In addition to use of the personal computer, with the commitment libraries are making to Internet technology and the extent to which they are thus attracting remote customers—as well as customers who visit the building—it makes sense to consider pursuing assessment using the Internet in appropriate ways.

How attuned are library decision makers to their customers' feelings about the service they receive?[9]

NOTES

1. Don A. Dillman, Robert D. Tortora, and Dennis Bowker, "Principles for Constructing Web Surveys" (1999), 1. Available (WebSurveyor): http://www.websurveyor.com/home_tips.asp.

2. *SPSS*, http://www.spss.com.

3. SurveyPro, from Apian Software, Inc., http://www.apian.com; Snap Professional, from Mercator Corp., http://www.mercatorcorp.com.

4. Scantron Corp., http://www.scantron.com; National Computer Systems, Inc., NCS Professional Survey System, http://www.ncs.com.

5. Remark Web Survey from Principia Products, Inc., http://www.principiaproducts.com.

6. Abstat, from Anderson-Bell Corp., http://www.andersonbell.com. Surveytools Corporation provides a version of Abstat that is preconfigured to analyze the satisfaction surveys described in this book.

7. Infopoll, Inc., Infopoll Server Software, http://www.infopoll.com; WebSurveyor Corp., WebSurveyor, http://www.websurveyor.com.

8. See, for example, products and services offered by Message Media, Inc., http://www.messagemedia.com.

9. Peter Hernon and Ellen Altman, *Service Quality in Academic Libraries* (Norwood, N.J.: Ablex, 1996), p. 111.

8

Analyzing Survey Results

Statistical procedures are basically methods of handling quantitative information in such a way as to make the information meaningful.[1]

The data collected from a survey for providing feedback on the service plan could be the result of either a quantitative or qualitative method of data collection. Quantitative methods involve measurement and "the process through which observations are translated into numbers."[2] Qualitative methods lack such specificity but can produce useful insights. A study may have both quantitative and qualitative aspects. Open-ended questions on a survey, for example, may ask for responses that will later be classified into general categories—ones that do not lend themselves to immediate measurement but that can be clustered and counted. As a result, questions such as "What do you like best about our service?" and "Name one thing we can do to improve" involve qualitative analysis because respondents are not selecting from a list of predetermined categories.

This chapter is intended as a guide to librarians and students who do not have a statistics background but who want to see how to analyze and present data gathered from an investigation of either service quality or satisfaction. Readers needing a more in-depth discussion of statistics should see works such as Ronald R. Powell's *Basic Research Methods for Librarians*,

Robert Swisher and Charles R. McClure's *Research for Decision Making: Methods for Librarians,* or Peter Hernon's *Statistics: A Component of the Research Process.*[3] In fact, figure 1-4 of Hernon's *Statistics* lists some excellent works on research methods and statistics from disciplines other than library and information science.

The chapter begins with an explanation of statistical terms. It then illustrates how to analyze statistical data based on examples of results from a library customer survey (figure 2.1) and from excerpts from customer satisfaction questionnaires (figures 6.2 and 6.3). Some readers may wish to refer to the examples in the section on Satisfaction Survey Analysis.

Clearly, libraries have a choice: They might engage in the use of probability sampling (selecting a sample that is representative of a population) or they might study respondents without being concerned about their representativeness of a population. Inferential statistics apply to the former instance and descriptive statistics to both. The presentation of the satisfaction questionnaires in this chapter focuses on descriptive statistics in the assumption that many academic and public libraries may lack the time and resources to engage in probability sampling. However, anyone wanting an example of how to draw a probability sample for a study of service quality should see Danuta A. Nitecki and Peter Hernon.[4]

Measurement Scales

Measurement, which assigns numbers to specify differing characteristics of a variable, provides a means for quantifying variables and making comparisons among them. A measurement scale follows a set of rules for assigning numerical scores to a variable. There are four types of measurement scales: nominal, ordinal, interval, and ratio.

Nominal Scales

The simplest of the four, nominal scale measurement, identifies or differentiates groups or objects by name without assuming any numerical order. Such measurement names mutually exclusive categories for groups or objects, but there is no inherent order to these categories; "mutually exclusive" signifies that an object can be assigned to only one category of a variable. Examples of nominal scale categories include gender; yes/no responses; a library customer's occupation or college or department, status (full- or part-time), class level, or student residency (on- or off-campus); types of library resources (e.g., books, journals, newspapers, and government publications); library departments (e.g., reference); geographical regions of the nation; and ZIP codes.

Ordinal Scales

The ordinal scale differentiates, ranks, and orders objects or groups from lowest to highest (or vice versa) according to some property or characteristic. Thus, it is possible to see whether a group or object falls into certain numerically ordered categories. Although the order of the category shows the relative position of something, that order does not indicate the extent of the difference between positions. In other words, the categories lie along a dimension, and, for example, a data point placed in category 1 is greater than a data point placed in category 2; a data point in category 2 exceeds one in category 3; and so forth. As a result, for example, "the ordinal scale measurement ranks of participants in a marathon but does not indicate how far ahead the first finisher was of the second or how far ahead the second finisher was of the third. These are distinctions that require the use of interval scale measures."[5] Examples of ordinal scale might be response categories of "never," "sometimes," "frequently," and "always"; age expressed as unequal units (e.g., 20–24, 25–28, 29–32, and over 32); or a Likert-type scale of intensity (e.g., "strongly disagree" to "strongly agree"). A Likert scale shows a differentiation among respondents who have a variety of opinions about something.

Interval Scales

Interval scales, like ordinal scales, differentiate and rank objects or groups, but they also require equal distance between categories. The range between the highest and lowest scores is divided into a number of equal units, like temperature measured on the Fahrenheit scale. As in the Fahrenheit scale, however, 0° has no absolute meaning; "Because of this fact . . . we cannot express the absolute ratio of two objects' magnitude of some property. We cannot say that today is four times 'hotter' than yesterday because the temperature yesterday was 4° and today's temperature is 16°. On the Fahrenheit scale of temperature 0° does not mean the absence of temperature."[6] As Ronald R. Powell notes, "interval level data are less common than ordinal in the social sciences."[7]

Ratio Scales

Ratio scales are interval scales with an absolute zero point. Examples include height and weight and a person's actual age or income, if the categorization permits the possibility of there being an absolute zero. In the social sciences, there are not many instances of ratio scales because few scales have an absolute zero and because respondents are less likely to disclose such information about themselves.

Point Scales Used for Surveys

Satisfaction and service quality surveys have tended to use a five- or seven-point scale for numeric scores. When librarians set goals and try to meet service targets to attain those goals, they might consider the use of a ten-point scale. Such a scale reflects incremental changes over time when used repeatedly, and it reflects the extent of progress in reaching service targets.

Evaluators might use the scale in conjunction with open-ended comments that the customer uses to explain his or her response to the scaled score. These customer comments offer concrete sentiments about the specific use of a service.

A ten-point scale is easily understood and avoids a numeric midpoint. The following bracketed ten-point scale is based on the familiar ten-point rating scale but is broken by brackets into five important sections that aid its interpretation. (Brackets are not necessary in the questionnaire.)

1 [2 3 4] [5 6] [7 8 9] 10

A respondent will focus on either the lower or upper half of the scale. The ten-point scale, in effect, becomes a five-point scale at either end, with the [7 8 9] grouping offering the respondent a way to fine-tune a nonextreme score. That is, a score of 7 indicates moderate satisfaction and signals that there is room for improvement without expressing actual dissatisfaction.

For example, "Overall, how satisfied are you with your college education to date?"

Scores of 1 and 10 are extremes; you cannot get worse or better than these. Therefore, few people probably choose either of these scores. On the one hand, a student who is paying more than $20,000 per year to receive a college education is not likely to admit complete dissatisfaction and remain at that institution. That student may not want to admit that his or her investment in the education received was worth nothing. On the other hand, a student may not be inclined to indicate complete satisfaction, perhaps at least not until securing a good job at a prestigious firm.

Scores of 5 and 6 generally indicate only slight dissatisfaction or satisfaction; however, selecting the 5 or 6 forces an inclination in one direction or the other. If someone feels strongly about an exact midpoint, he or she will write it in, mark the center point, or circle both the 5 and 6 together. (Similarly, a small number of people may mark positions between the other scores as well.) In such cases, the evaluator might enter the decimal midpoint (e.g., 5.5). If a software package accepts only integer data, enter the lower score, which is the more conservative value. (If respondents mark several noninteger values, alternatively enter the lower and higher scores.)

The [2 3 4] and [7 8 9] ranges indicate dissatisfaction and satisfaction, respectively. Most people will respond in these ranges. The particular usefulness of these ranges is that they allow the respondent to show degrees of general dissatisfaction or satisfaction. The 3 and 8 scores are midpoints within these ranges. People who score an 8 are indicating that they are quite happy, but that some things could still be better. An average score of at least 8 is very good, whereas people who score a 7 are indicating that they are not exactly dissatisfied, but that they are near the lowest range of satisfaction.

Scores below a 7 should be a cause of concern, but of greatest and most immediate concern are those who score in the 1 to 4 range. These responses are clearly signaling certain dissatisfaction. Imagine that the lower the score, the louder the voice of dissatisfaction.

Five-Point Scale

In comparison with the ten-point scale, the five-point scale is commonly used and preferred by some, especially when measuring slight changes over time is not required. Some people tend to avoid giving the extreme scores of 1 and 5. The 3 is an exact midpoint between satisfaction and dissatisfaction. That means that there is only one possible score to indicate general dissatisfaction or satisfaction, a 2 or 4, respectively. For a one-time survey, this may be all that is needed. For a repeated survey, however, evaluators want to detect possible incremental improvements in satisfaction over time. This is not possible with a five-point scale and less so with a four-point scale. Incidentally, it is easy to collapse scores from a ten-point to a five-point scale, but it is impossible to go the other way.

Seven-Point Scale

A seven-point "expectations" scale is the most direct means by which customers can indicate whether their expectations were met. For example, "Please indicate whether we fall short of, exactly meet, or exceed your expectations:"

A questionnaire could use both seven- and ten-point scales, depending on what the evaluators want to know. Note that unlike the ten-point scale, the seven-point scale has a midpoint, which is necessary to indicate that expectations are exactly met. In this case, offering a midpoint allows the customer to signal that expectations are being exactly met. (In contrast, it is not advised to offer customers an exact midpoint when measuring satisfaction because the goal is to measure whether the customer is *more* or *less* satisfied, in however small degree, and offering a midpoint as a response would, in effect, allow the customer to avoid answering the question.)

Also note that the ten-point scale used to measure satisfaction uses labels at each end that denote the extreme limits of dissatisfaction and satisfaction, respectively. In a complete spectrum, the use of 10 points is appropriate. In contrast, the expectations scale does not use end points that represent extreme positions, but shows a direction, either toward falling short of expectations or exceeding expectations. Here it is sufficient to offer up to three points in either direction adequately to capture the range of intensity of the respondent's opinion. Thus, whereas the ten-point scale covers the total spectrum of satisfaction and its absence, the seven-point scale, with zero as a midpoint, is adequate to indicate whether a respondent's expectations are more or less met.

Level of Significance

The level of significance is the predetermined level at which a null hypothesis (a hypothesis of no difference between the populations being compared) is not supported. The level is used to decide whether any change in a sample is likely to have resulted from chance. Common conventions in library and information science are probability (p) is less than or equal to .10, .05, and .01. Evaluators decide on the level prior to data collection after they have evaluated the consequences of making a Type I error (rejecting a true null hypothesis) or a Type II error (accepting a false null hypothesis as true).[8] They then either support or fail to support a null hypothesis on the basis of that level. To illustrate a null hypothesis, turn to figure 6.2, the satisfaction survey of the public library, and questions 2, 8, 11, and 12. Hypotheses become

there is no statistically significant difference (p = .05) in the age of the respondents (question 12) and the extent of their overall satisfaction with the library (question 2), or

there is no statistically significant difference (p = .05) between the frequency of public library use (question 11) and the primary reason for using the library (question 8).

If the probability level is set at p = .05, evaluators support the null hypothesis if the probability for the data collected exceeds .05; conversely, if the sample results produce a value equal to or less than .05, there is significance, and the null hypothesis is not supported. In other words, there likely is a difference.

Nonetheless, evaluators should exercise caution in interpreting statistical significance. The results, after all, may not be significant in social, practical, or policy terms. As a clarification, Powell notes, "differences of a few thousand volumes between two university library collections could produce significant statistical differences, but in terms of multimillion volume collections, such a difference holds little if any practical significance."[9]

Contrary to some research literature appearing in library and information science, there are no shades of statistical significance. Results, in other words, are not "somewhat," "moderately," or "highly" significant; rather, they are either significant or not significant. A determination that significance exists requires the use of statistical tests. Finally, evaluators should not look at the printout of results and let it dictate whether there is significance. Since an event unlikely to occur by chance is called "statistically significant," the term should be used with caution. The level of significance is set before data are collected, and the level selected is based on previous research, library policy, and the commitment of library resources and skilled staff to gather high-quality data.

Errors of Measurement and Classification

Research and measurement are susceptible to error. With some surveys, measurement and classification error may be insignificant, while in other instances error might seriously limit the types of conclusions that can be drawn from the data set. Although errors of measurement and classification are never totally eliminated, researchers try to minimize them and their impact on a study. Total error, which includes both sampling and nonsampling error, can be classified as

coverage errors, which result from inadequate sampling and low response rates

measurement errors, which are due to faulty data collection instruments, poor-quality interviewing, poor respondent recall, response errors, and mistakes in data processing (editing, coding, data entry, and data analysis)

sampling error, which is a function of the sample quality—whether a sample exactly represents a population

Error also results from misrepresentation. Misrepresentation might involve falsification, but it might also result from exaggeration. Some other potential sources of error include evaluator or sponsorship bias or faulty interpretation by the evaluator.[10]

Evaluators should pay close attention to issues of *reliability*, which relates to the stability and consistency of measurement (accuracy and replication), and to *internal validity*, which examines the extent to which the data measure what they purport to measure. For example, if library evaluators explore service quality and the satisfaction of customers with library services, internal validity relates to whether evaluators sufficiently understand what the concepts of service quality and satisfaction are and how well both concepts are represented in their data collection instruments. *Reliability* refers to the clarity of questionnaire items and the degree to which the data are consistent; *consistency* is the extent to which the same results are produced from different samples or at different times.

The Descriptive Presentation of Data

Descriptive statistics provide a useful and convenient means for summarizing data sets but not for generalizing the results from a sample to a population. A descriptive statistic is a number, computed from the responding observations, that in some way describes the group of cases. As Hubert M. Blalock Jr. explains,

> Quite frequently in social research a person will find himself in the position of having so much data that he cannot adequately absorb all his information. He

may have collected 200 questionnaires and be in the embarrassing position of having to ask, "What do I do with it all?" With so much information, it would be exceedingly difficult for any but the most photographic minds to grasp intuitively what is in the data. The information must somehow or other be boiled down to a point at which the researcher can see what is in it; it must be summarized. By computing measures such as percentages, means, standard deviations, and correlation coefficients it may be possible to reduce the data to manageable proportions.[11]

The following sections will highlight the most frequently used descriptive statistics that occur within the literatures of service quality and satisfaction. Descriptive statistics include ratios, frequency distributions and percentages, measures of central tendency, and measures of variability. Graphic representations of the data reflect data distribution patterns and highlight selected findings. Descriptive statistics depict the shape of a distribution.

Ratios

A ratio describes the relationship between two quantities mathematically. To obtain a ratio, divide one number (numerator) by another number (denominator).

$$\text{Ratio} = \frac{\text{Numerator}}{\text{Denominator}} = \underline{\qquad}$$

Input, output, and the other types of measures discussed in chapter 4 are expressed as ratios, and then are converted into percentages. For example, Paco Underhill, an environmental psychologist and researcher for Fortune 500 corporations, in his popular book *Why We Buy*, discusses waiting time and the importance of taking peoples' minds off how much time they must wait.[12] Waiting represents an opportunity to offer reading material that explains library services or how to gain access to information; thus, a hypothetical ratio and percentage could be

$$\text{Ratio} = \frac{\substack{\text{number in lines who are} \\ \text{reading library handouts}}}{\substack{\text{number of people} \\ \text{waiting in lines}}} = \underline{\qquad}\%$$

This ratio assumes that the staff have placed handouts nearby. Also assume that for one hour (when data are collected) 50 people stand in line and 30 of them pick up and read the handouts; the ratio is 30/50 or 60%.

Another example relates to a service pledge that customers will not stand in line longer than five minutes or additional staff will be called to the service area. Thus, researchers could determine the percentage of those customers waiting more than five minutes and the percentage of instances that additional staff appear when the five-minute limit is reached.

Frequency Distributions and Percentages

A frequency distribution is a tabulation or counting of responses. This count displays the frequency of occurrence and highlights patterns in the distribution of scores. A frequency distribution groups data into predetermined categories and reports numbers or scores for individual categories.

Statistics: A Component of the Research Process offers examples of frequency distribution and percentages.[13] Regarding a service quality or satisfaction survey, the data collected from any concluding question about respondent demographics (e.g., occupation, gender, and age) could be expressed in terms of frequencies and percentages.

Measures of Central Tendency

A measure of central tendency (an average, which can take three forms: the mode, mean, or median) "is an expression of the typical value of a distribution of scores; it is a generalization from all cases in a distribution to one value that is taken to be somewhat representative of all cases."[14] For examples showing how to calculate each type of average, see Arthur W. Hafner.[15] Hafner offers a set of discussion questions and problems to clarify the terms.

Returning to the scales used with either the service quality or satisfaction survey, the investigator will calculate the percentage of responses for each number (e.g., for "6," "7," and "8"). The researcher might, for instance, also produce a measure of central tendency that indicates the typical value for a set of observations (mean) or the most frequent value of a set of numbers (mode). The appendix at the end of this chapter explains when each type of average or measure of central tendency is appropriate.

Mode

The mode is the value that has the largest frequency in the distribution; therefore, it is the least stable. The mode is most likely to change from one sample of a population to another. If there are ties in the most frequently mentioned scores, multiple modes appear. The mode is most commonly employed with nominal variables but could be used with ordinal, interval, or ratio scales.

Mean

The mean, or the arithmetic average, is calculated by summing all the distribution's values together and dividing this sum by the number of cases in the distribution. "The mean value does not have to be a value actually found in the cases. Unlike the median, however, the mean is based on all of the values in the distribution."[16] The mean is important because evaluators can compare all individual scores with this number as being either above or below the mean. "The mean may not be a good choice if several cases are outliers or if the distribution is notably asymmetric. The reason is that the mean is strongly influenced by the presence of a few extreme values, which may give a distorted view of central tendency." In standard practice the mean applies to the interval and ratio but not to the nominal or ordinal scales.[17]

Median

The median considers only the value of the middlemost case. It divides the distribution in half.

> [The median] is a resistant measure. That means it is not much affected by changes in a few cases. Intuitively, this suggests that significant errors of obser-

vation in several cases will not greatly distort the results. Because it is a resistant measure, outliers have less influence on the median than on the mean. For example, notice that the observations 1, 4, 4, 5, 7, 7, 8, 8, 9 have the same median (7) as the observations 1, 4, 4, 5, 7, 7, 8, 8, 542. The means (5.89 and 65.11, respectively), however, are quite different because of the outlier 542 in the second set of observations.[18]

This example is merely illustrative. In practice, the 542 would probably be an error. The median can be used with ordinal, interval, and ratio scales but not with nominal scales.

Measures of Variability

Whereas an average defines a point around which other scores tend to cluster, measures of variability indicate how widely the scores are dispersed around the average. Such measures refer to the range, variance, and standard deviation. For examples of each and how to calculate and interpret the statistics, see Arthur W. Hafner; also see Charles H. Busha and Stephen P. Harter.[19]

Range

The range is the difference between the highest and lowest values in the distribution. It does not take into account the number of cases in the distribution. The range does not reflect variations in between the highest and lowest values or the nature of the spread around any measures of central tendency.

Variance and Standard Deviation

Measures of central tendency compress the different values for a variable into one value that represents a generalization about all of the values. Variance, on the other hand, measures the amount of dispersion, or spread of the values of cases, from the mean.

Like variance, the standard deviation measures the dispersion of scores around the mean. The standard deviation, which is the square root of the variance, uses data produced from the interval or ratio scale. When the data are normally distributed, about 68 percent of the scores fall within 1 standard deviation above and below the mean; and about 95 percent of the scores fall within 2 standard deviations above and below the mean. For a satisfaction survey, the standard deviation shows how much agreement there is among responses. This is useful information to know because the lower the standard deviation, the more agreement there is among respondents.

Graphing the Results

Graphing the data becomes an important way to see trends and to make comparisons. There are a number of types of charts or graphs:

Pie charts are circle charts that show the proportion of each variable to the whole expressed in percentages.

Scattergrams, or scatter charts, portray the distribution of findings as dots placed across the axes.

Histograms are bar graphs representing the frequency with which different values of a variable occur.

Line graphs, which are similar to frequency polygons, rely on each line to represent a different variable.

Area graphs take the line graph and shade the entire area between the axes and the connecting points on the line.

Bar graphs take many forms. A clustered bar graph displays two or more variables, and the bars are either vertical or horizontal. A stacked bar graph, on the other hand, includes two or more variables in one bar, with each segment of the bar representing different value labels.[20]

It is possible to mix types of graphs. A line graph, for example, might be superimposed on a bar graph.

Today, many software packages graphically display study results, thereby adding a visual dimension to data interpretation. Nonetheless, evaluators should be careful to minimize the distortion of results. As Edward R. Tufte explains, the graphic presentation of data should

depict the data

induce the audience to reflect on substance—the meaning of the data

avoid distorting that meaning

present many numbers in a small space

summarize large data sets and make them coherent

encourage visual comparisons among data elements

reveal the data at different levels of detail, from a broad overview to specific details

have a reasonably clear purpose (e.g., description, exploration, or tabulation)

be closely integrated with the statistical and verbal descriptions of a data set[21]

Everything on a graph should be clearly explained. Different symbols should be easily distinguishable from each other, and both the lettering and shading should be readable and distinctive. If a graph appears in color, those colors should be carefully selected and distinctive. Colors should not clash or detract from the effectiveness of the presentation. Furthermore, color-blind readers may be unable to distinguish shades of colors such as green. If staff produce black-and-white photocopies of colored graphs, gray tones that are produced may be indistinguishable.

Assume that, in response to a survey question for an examination of service quality, evaluators asked for customer expectations with the statement "I feel my belongings are safe at the library" and further assume that, on a ten-point scale (with 1 being "strongly disagree" to 10 being "strongly agree"), 78 hypothetical respondents checked the following responses:

Point on Scale	Number of Responses
10	29
9	25
8	14
7	3
6	2
5	2
4	3

In a list of numbers and corresponding percentages, it would be difficult to see and visualize trends. To help in this regard, figure 8.1 part A displays the seven categories indicated by respondents in the form of a bar graph. Part B of figure 8.1 displays the same data as a line graph, and part C is an area graph. Part D shows the same information in a pie chart, but the numbers are difficult to decipher because value labels (e.g., strongly agree) have not been assigned to the numbers from 4 to 10. Value label decisions should be made prior to data collection and should reflect the library's perspective on the interpretation of the forthcoming data set. Any response less than 7, however, would probably reflect some dissatisfaction.

The Chi-Square Test of Independence

When evaluators collect data that represent either nominal or ordinal measurements, they may cast the data in the form of a contingency table, where the columns represent categories of one variable, rows portray categories of a second variable, and entries in the cells indicate the frequencies of cases for a particular row and column combination. Cross tabulation (or cross tabs) in statistical analysis software produces these contingency tables to compare independent variables or questions—those involving nominal or ordinal measurement.

For example, for the hypothesis presented earlier in the chapter (there is no statistically significant difference [p = .05] between the frequency of public library use and the primary reason for using the library), we can construct the cross tabulation table shown in figure 8.2.

Once respondents have completed the survey in figure 6.2 and the data have been entered into the computer, researchers can see how many respondents indicated "personal pleasure" together with "first visit," "personal pleasure," or "daily," and so on. To address the hypothesis, cross tabulation uses the chi-square test of independence, a general nonparametric test that compares the frequencies of two or more responding groups. The chi-square test measures the differences between two independent groups for significance. A note of caution is in order: If there are cells (e.g., the box for "first visit" and "personal pleasure" in figure 8.2) with no

FIGURE 8.1
Examples of Charted Responses to Safety at the Library Question

A. Bar Graph

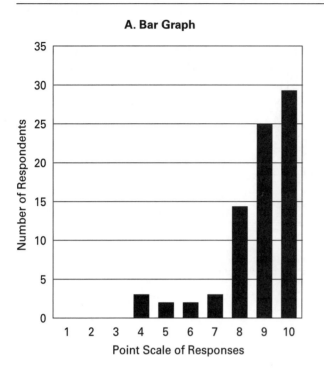

B. Line Graph

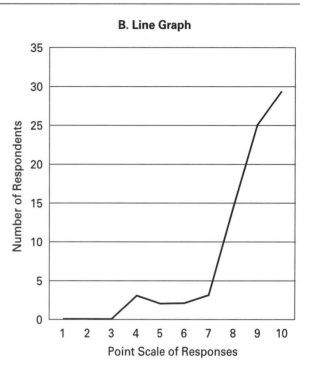

C. Area Graph

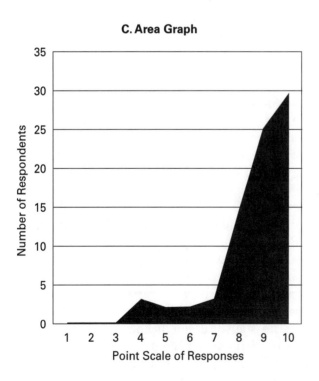

D. Pie Chart

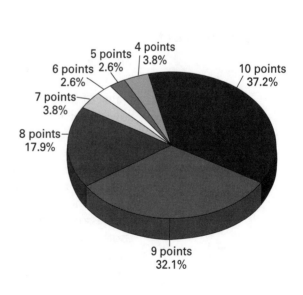

FIGURE 8.2

Sample Cross Tabulation of Primary Use of the Library with Frequency of Visits

Primary Use of the Library	How Often Use the Library							
	First visit	Daily	Weekly	Monthly	4 times/ year	2 times/ year	Once/ year	Less than once/year
Personal pleasure								
Personal research								
Work related								
School related								
Children's use								
Other								

responses or fewer than five responses, data analysis and hypothesis testing could be skewed. If this situation arises, see Hernon, *Statistics*.[22]

Strength of the Association

The *Phi coefficient* measures the strength of the association between two variables arrayed in a two-by-two (four-celled) contingency table. Phi assumes a value of 0 when no association exists. A value of +1 indicates a perfect, positive association, and a value of −1 means a perfect, negative association.

Cramer's V, a modified version of Phi, is suitable for contingency tables larger than two-by-two. The scale ranges from 0 to +1; the larger the value, the greater the association between the variables.

If the results of a cross tabulation indicate a significant difference, evaluators should turn to either Phi or Cramer's V to determine the strength of the association. In other words, the interpretation of findings addresses both statistical significance and strength of the association. Since the absence of a statistically significant difference between variables may comprise an important finding, evaluators should not fail to examine and report something for which there is no statistical significance. Sometimes, the most important findings relate to what was not significant.

Many statistical software packages calculate and report values for Phi and Cramer's V for any contingency table produced. Readers wanting more information about both correlation measures should consult *Statistics: A Component of the Research Process*.[23] Returning to figure 8.2, we see that the contingency table has eight columns for data and 6 rows. Thus, researchers expect to calculate a chi-square statistic and to see if that value is significant at $p = .05$. Assume that the value was significant but that the statistics software showed a value for Cramer's V of 0.158. This value is not large; thus, there is a statistically significant difference, but the strength of the association is not great. Researchers would, therefore, be cautious in their interpretation of the hypothesis. Clearly, use of Phi and Cramer's V encourage researchers to temper their interpretation of the hypothesis. Such statistics should be more widely used by researchers in library and information science when they use the chi-square test of independence.

Other Statistical Applications

In some instances, knowledgeable evaluators might use regression or factor analysis.[24] These are complex parametric tests that make explicit assumptions about population distributions. They assume that the phenomenon under investigation can be described by the means of normal distributions and that the population variances of comparison groups in a study are similar. A normal distribution assumes the shape of a symmetrical, bell-shaped curve. That bell-shaped curve extends infinitely in both directions in a continuum close to the horizontal axis, or baseline, but never touching it. The fact that the tails of the curve do not actually touch the baseline is not important because the area under the extreme ends (tails) is negligible. The most important feature of the curve is that it is symmetrical about its mean or central point. This signifies that if a normal curve were folded along its central line, the two halves of the curve would coincide.

When evaluators are investigating service quality and are engaged in gap analysis (see chapter 2), they might consider the use of quadrant analysis, a surprisingly simple-to-apply graphic correlation technique that produces an easily understood graphic and that identifies the most important findings.[25] *Assessing Service Quality* discusses quadrant analysis, a graphic correlation technique that produces a visualization of the data and those expectations of greatest importance to library customers.[26] Quadrant analysis involves the use of the mean for the expected scores (expectations that they would like any—ideal—library to meet). Then, the actual mean scores (expectations that a particular library meets), once calculated, are subtracted from the expected scores to produce a measure of the gap between the means. (See table 8.1.)

TABLE 8.1
Gap Analysis

Question	Mean Score (Expectations)	Mean Score (Actual Perceptions)	Gap between the Means
Materials in proper place	6.68	4.79	1.89
Staff available when needed	6.52	5.28	1.24

The quadrant analysis then displays the expected mean scores along the vertical axis and the gap scores along the horizontal axis. Only those expectations then falling into the first quadrant are very important to the customers, and they perceive the library as trying to meet those expectations.[27]

Clearly, quadrant analysis is useful when evaluators deal with gap analysis. If, however, they do not repeat the set of questions—if they ask only one set, the statements pertaining to the actual use of the library—evaluators cannot determine a gap. Rather, they calculate a mean, perhaps together with the standard deviation (if the mean is used) for each statement and display the results from highest to lowest scores. The question then becomes "How are the results interpreted objectively?" The library might conduct focus group interviews with the staff, seeing how they interpret the findings and where subjectivity enters the interpretation. Furthermore, assume a library has a customer service pledge that customers will stand in line for no more than five minutes. To evaluate whether the pledge has been met, evaluators examine the length of time that customers spend waiting in lines, perhaps by using a stop watch to see if the maximum time in the pledge has been reached.

The intent of the rest of this chapter is to pull together the discussion thus far in the chapter—to clarify the presentation of statistics. This chapter is not a substitute for the use of a statistics textbook, but it does present complex concepts and applications succinctly. To aid the reader unfamiliar with statistics, this section draws the discussion together with examples.

Library Customer Survey Analysis

Figure 2.1 presented a library customer survey that uses the ten-point scale. To that survey, we might add variables that describe respondents, such as their gender, age, or occupation.

The questions in section A of figure 2.1 involve the ten-point scale. Evaluators may decide to present the number and percentage for the numeric scores of each question in each set, but that information is less useful than the calculation of a measure of central tendency. Since past research on service quality and satisfaction has tended to regard the seven- or ten-point scales as interval measurement, most meaningful are the mean, mode, and standard deviation. The actual determination of which type of average to use depends on the measurement scale used and what the researchers want to know. (See the appendix at the end of this chapter.) Responses might also be presented in graphic form.

Additional Variables to Add to a Survey

At the end of figure 2.1, 6.2, or 6.3, we might include variables that describe respondents. Categories such as gender or occupation do not have an associated order (e.g., lowest to highest or highest to lowest). Thus, both questions involve labels or nominal measurement.

Examples of other satisfaction questions, those lending themselves to nominal measurement, include

Would you use the library again? _____ Yes _____ No

Would you recommend the library to your colleagues or friends?

_____ Yes _____ No

In analyzing the results, researchers might compare the variables that describe respondents, such as their gender and status. This comparison involves the display of two nominal scales in a contingency table. Thus, the appropriate statistical test becomes the chi-square test of independence, together with Cramer's V.

Assume that, once data were collected and inserted into a table depicting gender and status, a chi-square value of 1.96263 was calculated. Since the level of significance was set at $p = .05$, the next step is to determine the degrees of freedom (df), defined as the product of the number of columns and rows in the contingency table minus 1: $df = (c-1) \times (r-1)$. The degree of freedom is (2–1) for gender multiplied by (5–1) for status (undergraduate, graduate student, staff, faculty, and other), or 4.

Any statistics textbook contains an appendix of the chi-square distribution showing critical values of the statistic given levels of significance and degrees of freedom. An appendix would show that, for 4 df at $p = .05$, the critical value is 9.49. Because 1.96263 is less than 9.49, there is no statistically significant difference between status and gender. Males and females, in other words, are equally as likely to appear as a particular respondent status.

When using a statistical analysis software package, the computer automatically provides the df and the significance for the frequencies appearing in the table, so there is no need to consult the appendix of a statistics textbook. Since, in the example, no statistical difference emerged, there is no need to pay attention to the Cramer's V value.

If the survey instrument depicted in figure 2.1 asked respondents to complete an open-ended question as part of section C, evaluators would then read the comments and try to reduce the responses to useful categories. They might also want to pull out some comments to provide context and elaboration of the quantitative portion of the survey. For example, that survey might have contained questions such as:

- If any member of our staff provided you with outstanding service, please let us know.
- What do you like the best about the library?
- What do you like the least about the library?
- If we could only do one thing to improve, what should it be?

Progress toward Meeting Objectives and Customer Measures

A goal for satisfaction might be "in five years, fewer than 3 percent of respondents will express a score of less than 6 on the 10-point scale regarding their satisfaction with interlibrary loan service." An initial survey would indicate where the library stands in relation to the goal, and periodic surveys would assess progress toward reaching that target. Therefore, in the initial survey, the evaluators would focus on the frequency distribution and percentage. They might also present the data as, for example, a vertical or horizontal bar graph or a line graph. In the periodic survey they might also use frequency distributions, percentages, and graphs that deal with specific objectives and customer measures (see chapter 4). They might also use statistical procedures such as those discussed in this chapter.

Evaluators might also include an open-ended question to reinforce the results of the numeric portion of the survey. If both the quantitative and qualitative assessments indicate success (achievement of an 8 or higher and receive no negative comments), the organization should strive to maintain this level of performance in the future as it sets a new goal.

Satisfaction Survey Analysis

The satisfaction surveys presented in this book are best analyzed using methods that will paint a picture describing how satisfied the respondents are overall and with each of the dimensions; how satisfied they are according to how they use the library; what they feel are the best and worst things about the library; and what they recommend can be done to improve the library. To produce this picture, five methods are recommended:

a complete listing of all data

descriptive statistics

frequency counts presented with bar graphs

cross tabulations

open-ended question analysis using a cluster technique

The same methods can be used to analyze other variables in the questionnaire and respond to other questions about the data. The following examples are based on an analysis of the Public Library Customer Satisfaction Questionnaire (figure 6.2). A similar analysis would apply to the Academic Library Customer Satisfaction Questionnaire (figure 6.3), the Staff Satisfaction Questionnaire (figure 6.4), and the Workshop Evaluation Questionnaire (figure 6.6). The statistical software package used to generate these examples is Abstat (see chapter 7). Note that the examples are taken from various data sets, so there may not be consistency in the number of respondents or in the scores from sample to sample.

The Data Listing

A data listing is a complete listing of all data for each variable. Such a listing provides an easy way to proofread the data, a recommended first step in checking for possible data-entry errors and inappropriate responses by the survey respondents. The software should allow a selection of which variables to include in the listing so that evaluators can compare responses to two or more variables side-by-side. Table 8.2 lists data for the questionnaire number and the overall satisfaction and expectations variables for the first twenty-nine responses.

TABLE 8.2
Data List

Number	Overall	Expect	Number	Overall	Expect
1	10	3	16	9	2
2	9	2	17	8	0
3	8	0	18	7	0
4	5	−1	19	8	0
5	9	3	20	9	1
6	7	0	21	8	1
7	9	2	22	8	2
8	9	3	23	9	2
9	10	3	24	6	−1
10	8	2	25	7	0
11	—	—	26	8	1
12	3	−2	27	9	2
13	8	2	28	8	2
14	6	2	29	10	2
15	10	3			

The table shows twenty-nine responses, each response contained in a separate record. The "number" column lists the number assigned to each questionnaire as it was returned. (This makes it easy to locate a particular questionnaire after it is processed.) The variable names "overall" and "expect" represent overall satisfaction and expectations. The presentation of data in this format makes the proofreading process an easy first step and will provide greater confidence in the forthcoming analyses. For example, if a respondent rated overall satisfaction as 10, completely satisfied, it would be unlikely that the respondent would rate expectations as −3, fall short of expectations. If such ratings appeared, evaluators would want to check the original questionnaire responses to see if this was a data-entry error.

Descriptive Statistics

Descriptive statistics include a set of measurements that describe the group of respondents as a whole in terms of what is typical for the group—its central tendency. The specific descriptive statistics most useful for characterizing this central tendency include the mean, median, and mode. In addition, researchers will want to include the key statistic representing variability in responses—the standard deviation. These features characterize the group as a whole and allow one to compare individual responses to the group as being normal or higher or lower than normal. They are also useful metrics to compare one group of customers to other groups of customers and to track changes in a single group of customers over time. Descriptive statistics are, therefore, the most valuable set of characteristics used to understand responses to a survey.

Other items, such as minimum, maximum, and range, are self-explanatory. As mentioned previously, the key items of interest are the mean, median, mode, and standard deviation. These statistics are provided for each numeric variable in the database.

Mean

The mean shows the computed center point of the group, calculated by totaling the scores from each of the respondents and dividing the sum by the number of respondents who provided a score. This number is important because all individual scores can be compared with this number as being either above the mean, at the mean, or below the mean. However, the mean score itself, without reference to what individuals are saying in their open-ended responses, is not particularly useful to management except as an indicator. A comparison of means makes sense only when the same scale is used. For example, the overall satisfaction mean is based on a ten-point scale and the expectations mean is based on a seven-point scale, so these two means cannot be compared.

In the case of overall satisfaction, it will be useful to track the mean score over time to detect changes. However, far greater value may be found in responses to the open-ended question that asks, "If you are not satisfied, please explain why not" because responses to this question will give management specific suggestions on what needs to be improved. If such improvements are made, a higher average overall satisfaction score may result. The overall satisfaction score itself, therefore, is only an indicator.

Median

The median is simply the midpoint between the extreme scores in your group. We are less interested in the median as it applies to satisfaction surveys than in the mean and mode.

Mode

The mode reflects the score that most people chose. There may be no mode at all (as when everyone chooses a different score), and there may be multiple modes (when there are ties for the most frequently mentioned scores. Note in table 8.3 that the mean score for overall satisfaction is 8.25000, but the mode shows that more people rated overall satisfaction a 10 than any other score. Mean and mode are the principal ways to describe the central tendency of respondents to the satisfaction questionnaires.

Variance

The variance indicates how much variability is found in the scores as they are distributed around the mean. However, the variance is of less importance to note than the standard deviation, which is computed from the variance.

Standard Deviation

The standard deviation shows how much agreement there is among respondents who answered that question. This is a useful number to understand. The lower the standard deviation, the more agreement there is among respondents. The agreement can be confirmed visually by checking a graph of the frequency distribution.

Table 8.3
Key Descriptive Statistics

Variable	Valid Records	Number Missing	% Missing		Variable	Mean	Std. Dev.	Variance
OVERALL	20	0	0.0		OVERALL	8.25000	1.83174	3.35526
EXPECT	20	0	0.0		EXPECT	5.30000	1.55935	2.43158
PERIODICALS	20	0	0.0		PERIODICALS	7.95000	1.60509	2.57632

Variable	Minimum	Maximum	Range		Variable	Median	Mode
OVERALL	3	10	7		OVERALL	9.00000	10
EXPECT	1	7	6		EXPECT	5.50000	5
PERIODICALS	4	10	6		PERIODICALS	8.00000	7

Frequency Counts

A frequency count shows how many people answered a question using a particular response score or category. In addition to the counts, it is helpful to view the distribution of responses graphically, as in a horizontal bar graph. Table 8.4 displays the responses to the overall satisfaction question.

Overall Satisfaction

To examine overall satisfaction, a frequency distribution of the scores for that variable is prepared. In addition to the mean (8.04 in table 8.4) and standard deviation for the variable, a horizontal bar graph can provide a visual distribution of scores and also show the mode (the most frequently chosen score). Table 8.4 shows a fairly high level of satisfaction. Notice that the majority of responses are in the 8 and 9 categories. Note also the number of respondents who score below a critical threshold, such as 5 or 6. (In table 8.4, the cumulative percent column shows that responses of 7 and lower account for 25 percent of the scores in this example.) The software

TABLE 8.4
Frequency of Overall Satisfaction Scores

	Count	%	Adj. %	Cum. %
1	0	0.0	0.0	0.0
2	0	0.0	0.0	0.0
3	1	3.4	3.6	3.6
4	0	0.0	0.0	3.6
5	1	3.4	3.6	7.1
6	2	6.9	7.1	14.3
7	3	10.3	10.7	25.0
8	9	31.0	32.1	57.1
9	8	27.6	28.6	85.7
10	4	13.8	14.3	100.0
Total	28	96.6	100.0	100.0

Mean = 8.04
n of Mean = 28
Std. Dev. = 1.59820

should allow you to filter all responses with an overall satisfaction score below, say, a 5, and list the questionnaire numbers for those responses. It will then be possible to locate the original questionnaires and to read them more closely to determine possible causes for dissatisfaction. Of course, if the questionnaires were signed, it would also be possible to contact the customer to discuss and/or correct any problem.

If the satisfaction survey is conducted again in the following year or two, it will be instructive to compare the mean scores to see if there is a change and, if so, in which direction and by how much. Unlike the median score (which is simply a midpoint in the range of responses), the mean score will most likely reveal changes in either direction because it is calculated to take into account all of the actual scores. In any case, recall that the overall satisfaction score is just a number, an indication of how satisfied the group of respondents is, whereas the responses to the open-ended question asking why people are dissatisfied provide management with the truly important details worth addressing.

Note that in table 8.4, 28 customers answered this question; however, 29 customers returned the questionnaire, meaning that one customer did not answer this question. This explains the difference between the percentage distributions (96.6 in the % column) and the adjusted percentage distributions (100.0 in the adj. % column).

Expectations Scores

The next item of interest is the expectations score. Again, it is important to look first at the distribution of these scores using a frequency distribution. If expectations are being appropriately set and if these expectations are being met, it would not be surprising to see scores of zero for this scale. If expectations are being exceeded, scores above zero result. Table 8.5 shows that the

TABLE 8.5
Frequency of Expectations Scores

	Count	%	Adj. %	Cum. %
−3 Fall Short of Expectations	0	0.0	0.0	0.0
−2	1	3.4	3.6	3.6
−1	2	6.9	7.1	10.7
0 Exactly Meet Expectations	6	20.7	21.4	32.1
+1	3	10.3	10.7	42.9
+2	11	37.9	39.3	82.1
+3 Exceed Expectations	5	17.2	17.9	100.0
Total	28	96.6	100.0	100.0

Mean = 1.29
n of Mean = 28
Std. Dev. = 1.38396

mean is 1.29, which on this scale means that responses are above "exactly meets expectations." Note also that three customers indicated that their expectations were not being met. Again, for management purposes, it is of prime concern to focus on customers who indicate that expectations are not being met.

Dimensions Counts

The next example of a frequency count is the set of dimensions rated by the respondents. These dimensions are analyzed using a frequency distribution and noting the mean scores for each. Table 8.6 shows a frequency distribu-

TABLE 8.6
Frequency of Adult Books Scores

	Count	%	Adj. %	Cum. %
1	0	0.0	0.0	0.0
2	0	0.0	0.0	0.0
3	0	0.0	0.0	0.0
4	0	0.0	0.0	0.0
5	2	6.9	6.9	6.9
6	2	6.9	6.9	13.8
7	1	3.4	3.4	17.2
8	10	34.5	34.5	51.7
9	11	37.9	37.9	89.7
10	3	10.3	10.3	100.0
Total	29	100.0	100.0	100.0

Mean = 8.21
n of Mean = 29
Std. Dev. = 1.31961

tion for one dimension—adult books. All dimensions may be ranked according to descending mean score, but this is not necessary. It is more pertinent to note simply which dimensions are drawing the lowest scores because these may indicate the areas most in need of management attention for improvement. It can also be valuable to check whether any dimensions with low scores are also mentioned in the open-ended responses asking for reasons for dissatisfaction.

Cross Tabulations

A cross tabulation is a method of comparing responses using two variables at a time. Following are discussions of various cross tabulations. In addition to these, examine cross tabulations of overall satisfaction and expectations and of overall satisfaction and overall importance.

Primary Use Cross Tabulation

The primary use analysis is key to segmenting the customer base. It is instructive to prepare a cross tabulation of all variables by primary use. Looking at such a cross tabulation against overall satisfaction, in particular, will reveal whether some groups of users may be more or less satisfied. The mean scores for each use category can be compared, and management may then wish to focus on the lower scores to see how they might be improved. In table 8.7, 19 respondents use the library for personal pleasure, and their mean overall satisfaction score is 8.21 on a ten-point scale. Note the letter "C" in the left column indicates that the percentages are computed for the scores by column. For example, 16 percent of the respondents who use the library for personal pleasure gave an overall satisfaction score of 10.

Ease of Use and Overall Satisfaction Cross Tabulation

The ease of use analysis begins with a frequency distribution. Then it can be helpful to cross tabulate ease of use and overall satisfaction to see whether lower satisfaction scores may be related to lower ease of use scores. If primary use (the preceding variable) were cross tabulated with all variables, studying the results for ease of use will show which groups that use the library for particular purposes have the most or least difficulty. Pay special attention to scores below 7.

Library Member Cross Tabulation

The variable for library member should be cross tabulated with all variables. This will reveal how scores might be different depending on membership status. It is possible that through the membership process members are better apprised of the expectations the library wishes to set. It is also possible that nonmembers, particularly those coming from distant locations (as indicated by ZIP code), may value the library for something specifically important to them.

TABLE 8.7

Cross Tabulation of Primary Use of the Facility with Overall Satisfaction

			PRIMARY USE OF FACILITY					
			Personal pleasure	Personal research	Work related	School related	Children's use	Other
Overall Satisfaction								
1		0						
	C	0%						
2		0						
	C	0%						
3		1	1					
	C	3%	5%					
4		0						
	C	0%						
5		1			1			
	C	3%			50%			
6		2	2				1	
	C	7%	11%				5%	
7		3		1		1	2	
	C	10%		14%		100%	10%	
8		9	6	4			7	
	C	31%	32%	57%			35%	
9		8	7	1			7	
	C	28%	37%	14%			35%	
10		4	3	1	1		2	
	C	14%	16%	14%	50%		10%	
Total								
Respondents		29	19	7	2	1	20	
	C	100%	100%	100%	100%	100%	100%	
Mean		8.04	8.21	8.29	7.50	7.00	8.37	0.00
n of Mean		28	19	7	2	1	19	0
Std. Dev.		1.5982	1.6859	0.9512	3.5355	0.0000	1.0116	0.0000

Frequency of Visit Cross Tabulations

The frequency of visit variable may be analyzed first using a frequency distribution and then cross tabulated with overall importance, primary use, and town or ZIP code. Management may wish to pay more immediate attention to customers who use the library more frequently, particularly those whose satisfaction scores are low. The cross tabulations will also show what the primary uses of the library are according to those who are frequent or infrequent visitors and whether the infrequent visitors may be coming from a greater distance than those who visit more frequently.

Age Variable Cross Tabulations

The age variable is an important one because it can indicate quite different service needs for different customer age groups. Again, the frequency distribution is helpful, followed by a cross tabulation by overall importance, primary use, ease of use, and frequency of visit. Low ease-of-use scores among older users could indicate that they may benefit from special assistance. Older customers with a low frequency of visits might welcome efforts by the library to arrange for more convenient transportation to the library.

Open-Ended Analysis

The most valuable information in a survey may be found in the open-ended responses, in which respondents use their own words to answer a question. Such responses do not lend themselves to easy analysis, even using a computer. In fact, it is not advisable to use a statistical package to analyze open-ended responses. Instead, any standard word processor can provide the necessary functionality to put such responses in an easy-to-understand order. The procedure for this is called "cluster analysis." First, manually check the questionnaires to see that there are at least some similarities in the responses to an open-ended question. That is, if every respondent truly says something totally different, there's no basis for grouping responses. If there are commonalities, even though worded differently, cluster analysis will result in grouping such commonalities in an ordered manner. To begin, enter all the responses into a word processor, using a carriage return after each response. This provides a list of all the answers to one question.

Next, use the "sort" feature of the word processor to reorganize these answers alphabetically. It becomes immediately apparent if some respondents are using the same first word in their responses. Next, read each response in the list to see how various wordings can be clustered under the same category. For example, the following responses could be clustered under the standard term "maintenance":

> reading chairs are in disrepair
>
> some of the numeric signs on the stacks are missing
>
> the north entrance needs shoveling after it snows

Based on common responses, prepare a list of standard terms. The terms used will be the basis for sorting responses, so it is useful to select terms that are of specific interest to management. Enter the standard term in front of each response of its type, and use a colon to separate the standard term from the corresponding phrase.

> maintenance: reading chairs are in disrepair
>
> maintenance: some of the numeric signs on the stacks are missing
>
> maintenance: the north entrance needs shoveling after it snows

Repeat the alphabetical sort function, and all the maintenance problems will be clustered together. Next move on to the category "organizational problems," and so forth, using the appropriate standard term for that cluster. When completed, an organized picture will emerge that makes it much easier to visualize how respondents feel.

Manually count the number of responses for each standard term to see how many people are mentioning the same issue. When doing this, it is important to bear in mind that only one or two individuals may be making comments that are extremely important. Sometimes only one respondent has an insight that, while not mentioned by anyone else, is a gem of a suggestion. This emphasizes the need to read every response and not to focus only on those with the largest aggregate counts.

It may seem simpler to compile a thesaurus of cluster terms and dispense with the tedium of entering all open-ended responses in their entirety. While this is a choice left up to the evaluator, such an abbreviated approach can compromise the value of the analysis because a single term used for grouping purposes may not adequately convey the intended message.

The open-ended responses to the last question on figure 6.2, which asks for any other comments or suggestions, may be either positive, negative, or a combination. It can be helpful to add an additional code or indicator of whether the response is positive or negative or contains both positive and negative elements. Totaling the positive and negative codes reveals the overall sentiment of the group.

Summary

Some excellent textbooks review the types of statistics discussed in this chapter and illustrate step-by-step how to calculate them.[28] Such works provide insights into descriptive and inferential (using data from a sample to project to the population) statistics. Those evaluators unfamiliar with such tests should consult these works prior to engaging in computer analysis.

At the same time, it is important to realize that qualitative methods, including those related to analyzing open-ended responses, provide useful insights. Nonetheless, overuse of open-ended questions or a lengthy and poorly constructed questionnaire will produce a low response rate, and the survey will have severe data-quality problems.

Finally, any research (evaluation or other type of study) must pass a "truth test" and a "utility test." The former test asks, "Is the research trustworthy, can I rely on the findings, and will it hold up under attack?" The latter test raises the questions "Does the research provide direction [and] does it provide guidance?"[29]

The research process is a tool to assist in library decision making and planning.[30]

NOTES

1. Donald Ary, Lucy C. Jacobs, and Asghar Razavieh, *Introduction to Research in Education*, 3rd ed. (New York: Rinehart and Winston, 1985), 95.

2. Ibid.

3. Ronald R. Powell, *Basic Research Methods for Librarians*, 3d ed. (Greenwich, Conn.: Ablex, 1997); Robert Swisher and Charles R. McClure, *Research for Decision Making: Methods for Librarians* (Chicago: American Library Assn., 1984); Peter Hernon, *Statistics: A Component of the Research Process* (Norwood, N.J.: Ablex, 1994).

4. Danuta A. Nitecki and Peter Hernon, "Measuring Service Quality at Yale University's Libraries," *Journal of Academic Librarianship*, 26 (July 2000), 259–73.

5. Arthur W. Hafner, *Descriptive Statistical Techniques for Librarians*, 2d ed. (Chicago: American Library Assn., 1998), 11.

6. Swisher and McClure, *Research for Decision Making*, 78.

7. Powell, *Basic Research Methods for Librarians*, 43.

8. See Hernon, *Statistics*, 115–17.

9. Powell, *Basic Research Methods for Librarians*, 199.

10. Ibid., 82–6.

11. Hubert M. Blalock Jr., *Social Statistics* (New York: McGraw-Hill, 1972), 4.

12. Paco Underhill, *Why We Buy: The Science of Shopping* (New York: Simon & Schuster, 1999), 189–94.

13. Hernon, *Statistics*, 83–8.

14. Swisher and McClure, *Research for Decision Making*, 135.

15. Hafner, *Descriptive Statistical Techniques for Librarians*, 127–68.

16. Swisher and McClure, *Research for Decision Making*, 137.

17. U.S. General Accounting Office, *Quantitative Data Analysis*, 31.

18. U.S. General Accounting Office, Program Evaluation and Methodology Div., *Quantitative Data Analysis: An Introduction* (Washington, D.C.: The Office, 1992), 32.

19. Hafner, *Descriptive Statistical Techniques for Librarians*, 171–3 (range), 181–8 (standard deviation); Charles H. Busha and Stephen P. Harter, *Research Methods for Librarianship: Techniques and Interpretation* (New York: Academic Press, 1980), 236–40 (variance).

20. Powell and Hafner discuss some of the types of graphs. See Powell, *Basic Research Methods for Librarians*, 183–90; Hafner, *Descriptive Statistical Techniques for Librarians*, 86–118. Other examples can be found in Hernon, *Statistics*, 90–3.

21. Edward R. Tufte, *The Visual Display of Quantitative Information* (Cheshire, Vt.: Graphics Press, 1983), 13.

22. Hernon, *Statistics*, 141–2.

23. Hernon, *Statistics*, 147–50.

24. Ibid., 189–200.

25. Hernon and Altman, *Assessing Service Quality*, 198–204. For a clear analysis of how to apply gap analysis, see Nitecki and Hernon, "Measuring Service Quality at Yale University's Library."

26. Ibid., 198–202.

27. Ibid., 201.

28. See Powell, *Basic Research Methods for Librarians;* Hafner, *Descriptive Statistical Techniques for Librarians;* Hernon, *Statistics;* Stephen Isaac and William B. Michael, *Handbook in Research and Evaluation,* 3d ed. (San Diego, Calif.: EdiTS, 1995), 184–9.

29. Carol H. Weiss and Michael J. Bucuvalas, "Truth Tests and Utility Tests: Decision-Makers' Frames of Reference for Social Science Research," *American Sociological Review* 45, no. 2 (April 1980): 302–3.

30. Swisher and McClure, *Research for Decision Making,* 100.

APPENDIX

Illustrative Measures of Central Tendency

To illustrate some considerations involved in determining the central tendency of a distribution, we can . . . assume that a questionnaire has been sent to . . . 800 Social Security recipients, asking how satisfied they are with program services. Further, imagine four hypothetical distributions of the responses. By assigning a numerical value of 1 to the item response "very satisfied" and 5 to "very dissatisfied," and so on, we can create an ordinal variable. The three measures of central tendency can then be computed to produce the results in the . . . [accompanying table]. Although the data are ordinal, we have included the mean for comparison purposes.

Attribute	Distribution			
	A	**B**	**C**	**D**
Very satisfied (1)*	250	250	100	159
Satisfied (2)	200	150	150	159
Neither satisfied nor dissatisfied (3)	125	0	300	164
Dissatisfied (4)	125	150	150	159
Very dissatisfied (5)	100	250	100	159
Total responses	800	800	800	800
Mean	2.5	3	3	3
Median	2	3	3	3
Mode	1	1 and 5	3	3

*The number in parentheses refers to the numerical value for each attribute.

In distribution A, the data are distributed asymmetrically. More persons report being very satisfied than any other condition, and the mode of 1 reflects this. However, 225 beneficiaries expressed some degree of dissatisfaction (codes 4 and 5), and these observations pull the mean to a value of 2.5 (that is, toward the dissatisfied end of the scale). The median is 2, between the mode and the mean. Although the mean might be acceptable for some ordinal variables, in this example it can be misleading and shows the danger of using a single measure with an asymmetrical distribution. The mode seems unsatisfactory also because, although it draws attention to the fact that more respondents reported satisfaction with the services than any other category, it obscures the point that 225 reported that they were dissatisfied or very dissatisfied. The median seems a better choice for this distribution if we can display only one number, but showing the whole distribution is probably wise.

In distribution B, the mean and the median both equal 3 (a central tendency of "neither satisfied not dissatisfied"). Some would say this is nonsense in terms of the actual distribution, since no one actually chose the middle category. The modes 1 and 5 seem the better choices to present the clearly bimodal distribution, although again a display of the full distribution is probably the best option.

In distribution C, the mean, median, and mode are identical; the distribution is symmetrical. Any one of the three ways would be appropriate. One easy check on the symmetry of a distribution, as this shows, is to compare the values of the mean, median, and mode. If they differ substantially, as with the distribution A, the distribution is probably such that the median should be used.

As distribution D illustrates, however, this rule-of-thumb is not infallible. Although the mean, median, and mode agree, the distribution is almost flat. In this case, a single measure of central tendency could be misleading, since the values 1, 2, 3, 4, and 5 are all about equally likely to occur. Thus, the full distribution should be displayed.

The lesson of this example? First, before representing the central tendency by any single number, evaluators need to look at the distribution and decide whether the indicator would be misleading. Second, there will be occasions when displaying the results graphically or in tabular form will be desirable instead of, or in addition to, reporting statistics.

SOURCE: U.S. General Accounting Office, Program Evaluation and Methodology Division, *Quantitative Data Analysis: An Introduction* (Washington, D.C.: The Office, 1992), 33–6.

9

The Challenges to Being Successful

We understand the world by asking questions and searching for answers. Our construction of reality depends on the nature of our inquiry.[1]

Organizations are facing more intense customer service pressures than ever before.[2]

Customer service has been characterized in the literature as staff compliance with a few simple adages, such as "remember that the customer is not the enemy," "create a climate in your library that supports change," "survey the environment continuously," "redirect resources," and "treat every customer like a person."[3] Customer service has also been cast in terms of problem patrons and how to cope with them. Further adages relate to choosing new services, when librarians should consider five easy questions: "Do you have the skills? Do you have the time? Do you have the resources? Is it [the service] difficult to manage? Can it be abused?"[4] Being successful—providing high-quality services that satisfy or delight customers on a regular basis—means more than compliance with a few adages and questions that lack a planning context. Success involves the development, implementation, evaluation, and *ongoing updating* of a service plan that expresses realistic expectations, that the administration and staff are willing to commit the necessary resources to achieving, and that is truly meaningful to a library's customers. The *service plan* must be consistent with the library's vision and mission statements and its goals and objectives; and it must also enjoy broad customer and stakeholder support.

Service Quality and Satisfaction

The number of issues and problems that libraries could address is endless and deals, for instance, with accountability (e.g., the effectiveness, efficiency, value, and worth of library services, perhaps expressed in cost terms) and with the anticipated and actual amount of use (e.g., how long should libraries support a specific electronic service before deciding whether to continue that commitment). Another issue relates to quality, a multifaceted concept that can be viewed from different (but not necessarily mutually exclusive) perspectives: those of the library, broader organization or institution, or customer. For the customer, quality centers on the fulfillment of expectations.

Service quality has traditionally been viewed in terms of gap analysis, the extent of a gap between ideal and actual service expectations. Satisfaction, defined as the service provided minus the customer's expectations, offers a complementary view. Together, service quality and satisfaction represent the customer's perspective on quality.

In an important study, Patricia A. Knowles, Stephen J. Grove, and Gregory M. Pickett reported the impact of a customer's mood on service encounters. They found that

> Mood plays a less significant role than the nature of the service encounter itself when it comes to individuals' cognitive, affective, and conative responses. Furthermore, it appears that encounters containing positive aspects have the potential to overcome a negative mood state that customers may bring to a service interaction. . . . [As a result,] negative encounters—ones in which the personnel, the physical environment, and/or the service process combine to generate failure—have the potential to undermine customers' memory, evaluation, and behavior intentions regarding the service provider.[5]

They found that by paying attention to service quality and customer satisfaction staff may be able to sway a bad mood that the customer brings to a service encounter, thereby producing a positive service experience. The authors issue an important caveat: "Service managers may wish to avoid the inclination to elevate customers' . . . performance moods because it may be difficult to produce a service performance that is consistent with the customer's state. In this case, the adage, 'underpromise and overdeliver' takes on a special significance."[6] It becomes all the more essential that libraries, like any service organization, "emphasize those dimensions of service delivery on which the organization consistently performs well [and] enhance customers' recall of them [those dimensions]."[7]

As discussed in chapter 1, a library's vision guides which expectations the organization can (or will choose to) meet. This is not to say that customer expectations determine the vision or that library services should meet whatever expectations arise. Over time, customer expectations will change, and customers will make more demands on the service provided. Libraries therefore need to monitor changing expectations and see which ones they are prepared to meet. They should also identify and explain those they are unable to meet, as these might be beyond their control or ability to influence. They should also monitor the services that their competitors offer, seeing what they might adopt or adapt.

Central to this chapter and the book is the belief that different institutions and organizations likely have different service emphases, and attention to service quality begins with a localized prioritizing of areas for service improvement as defined by the library and those to whom the library director reports and as refined by customers. Thus, any comparison of service quality and satisfaction data across library settings could produce misleading and incomplete findings that are linked neither to strategic planning nor to a diagnosis of customer service. The intent is to take the library's temperature and to use the results for improving service provision and delivery within the context of that library's mission and vision.

Some Trends Likely to Change Expectations

The number and diversity of library competitors will likely increase, and these competitors will offer varied services that cater to customers and their expectations. For instance, Andrew Odlyzko, a researcher at AT&T Labs in New Jersey, when discussing large commercial and learned society publishers, argues that the conversion of scholarly journals to a digital format offers the best hope for their survival. He maintains that "the infamous 'journal crisis' is more of a library cost crisis than a publisher pricing problem, with internal library costs much higher than the amount spent on purchasing books and journals." He believes that publishers might be able to "retain or even increase their revenues and profits while providing superior service. To do this, they will have to take over many functions of libraries, and they can do that only in the digital domain."[8] If publishers "succeed in disintermediating the libraries and preserving their revenues," they will further alter scholarly communication and encourage "nontraditional methods of disseminating information (preprints . . . [in disciplines other than the physical sciences]), but also e-mail, Web pages, and so on."[9]

Undoubtedly, some new services, not necessarily offered by libraries, will be aimed at those individuals with advanced reading skills who can comprehend complex text, whereas other services will be targeted at those with lesser reading and comprehension skills. Improving the reading, communication, comprehension, and information literacy skills of students and the general public may well require a partnership among academic and public libraries, school media centers, corporations, government (federal, state, and local), and private sector vendors. Parents must also play a central role in this broad educational effort.

Interestingly, the public, according to reporter Will Weissert, who announced a report on "why the public loves higher education and criticizes K–12," has an image of academic institutions as located on "lush" campuses, with extensive library collections and where access to buildings does not require passing through metal detectors. Furthermore, institutional violence on those campuses is less prevalent, and "college students are forced to show individual initiative to succeed on campus and must pay for their own educations." As Weissert further reports, the business world is "less impressed by the way colleges operate."[10] Perhaps the business view is shaped by the products of academe whom they are asked to employ.

As this example indicates, stakeholders as well as customers may demand that the educational system, from kindergarten through college, perform better and meet a more diverse set of expectations. As well, libraries, especially academic and public libraries, may want to seek out and serve never-gained customers and some so-called lost customers, and enable them to become more self-sufficient and delighted library customers.

Changing Demographics

The United States is a multicultural, multilingual country that has an aging population. As the following section indicates, the complex picture that emerges will surely lead to new customer expectations. Clearly, expectations are not homogeneous across the population, and neither service quality nor customer satisfaction deals with a static set of expectations.

From July 1, 1995, to August 1, 1999, the age of the American population has increased from a median of 34.4 to 35.5 and from a mean of 35.8 to 36.4.[11] Based on projections by the Bureau of the Census for the period July 1, 2001, to July 1, 2005, the population age median and mean will continue to rise. Yet, the median age for people of color has lagged behind the numbers for the 1995–1999 period.[12] There is also likely to be a rapid rate of growth of the elderly (65 years or older) and especially the oldest-old (85 years or older) populations in the early twenty-first century as the post–World War II baby boom cohorts become elderly.

Another trend is that

> Between 1960 and 1980, the number of Americans who worked at home steadily declined, largely reflecting a drop in the number of family farmers who elected to give up farming. But . . . [more recently, there has been an] increase in the number of people who worked at home, up 56 percent from 1980, to 3.4 million people [1990]. . . . Given the advancements in personal computers and Internet technology since these data were collected in the 1990 census, we expect even more significant increases in the proportion working at home by Census 2000. . . .
>
> The primary difference between those who worked at home and those who worked away from home was the source of employment. More than half of the workers who labored in their homes . . . were self-employed in 1990, 10 times the rate of self-employment found among those who worked away from home. . . . For the work-at-home group, the proportion of women . . . was greater than for those who work away from home. . . . Those who worked at home were also older on average than those who did not.[13]

Turning to educational attainment in the United States, the Bureau of the Census reported, in one of its 1998 *Current Population Reports*, that about 82.2 percent of all adults ages 25 and over have completed high school and 24.4 percent have completed a bachelor's degree or more

the high school completion level of young adults (ages 25 to 29) was 88.1 percent, while the college completion level was 27.3 percent

among women 25 and over, 82.9 percent have earned a high school diploma, and 22.4 percent have completed a bachelor's degree or more

college completion rates for young women exceeded those for young men, 29.0 versus 25.6 percent, respectively, for those aged 25 to 29

for whites 25 and over, 83.7 percent completed high school and 25.0 percent have a bachelor's degree or more

annual average earnings for those age 18 and over in 1997 who only completed high school was $22,895; for those with a bachelor's degree, it was $40,478

about 89.5 percent of the employed civilian labor force aged 25 and over had a high school degree.[14]

These general findings have some significant exceptions; for instance, millions of individuals who have low skill levels and live in inner cities are jobless or stuck in low-paying, dead-end jobs. Furthermore, many jobs have moved from the cities to the suburbs, and these inner-city individuals may not be able to secure the kind of employment that might provide them with better chances of success. The educational and skill requirements for many jobs might be beyond them, and they do not qualify for most jobs that require basic computer literacy and reading, numeracy, and social skills—even at the entry level.

The high school drop-out rate is relatively stable at 5 percent. "This means that some 500,000 young people are still short-changing their lives and dropping out," stated U.S. Secretary of Education Richard W. Riley. In 1996, 9 percent of Hispanics left school before completing a high school program, compared with 6.7 percent for African Americans and 4.1 percent for Caucasians.[15]

A startling observation is that "more than 20 percent of adults read at or below a fifth-grade level," and "forty-three percent of people with the lowest literacy skills live in poverty; 17 percent receive food stamps, and 70 percent have no job or a part-time job."[16]

As these examples indicate, the amount of library use may increase for some groups and decrease or remain the same for other groups. At the same time, public libraries may need a broader array of resources aimed at a population that does not read much (is becoming more visually focused) or cannot read beyond elementary school. Academic libraries may require more resources for those in remedial education. Clearly, it is impossible to develop one set of expectations to serve an entire community or even the range of library customers. The survey instruments presented in previous chapters might require modification before being given to particular segments of the population, and surveys, especially mailed ones, may be inappropriate for some populations. Cheryl Metoyer-Duran offers guidance for anyone attempting to survey communities in which adults, as well as their offspring, may have no or limited ability to speak and write English.[17]

Reading Scores

The Department of Education has produced report cards on the nation's youth. The 1998 reading report card indicates that the national average reading score increased in grades 4, 8, and 12 but that

> Increased scores were not observed for all students. At grade 4, score increases were observed only among lower performing students. At grade 8, score increases were observed among lower and middle performing students. At grade 12, score increases were observed among middle and upper performing students; however, the score for lower performing twelfth graders was not as high in 1998 as it had been in 1992.[18]

Some of the other general findings from this report card are

> Female students had higher average reading scores than their male peers, and the percentage of females attaining each of the reading achievement levels exceeded that of males.

> At all three grades in 1998, the average reading score for white students was higher than that for African American, Hispanic, and American Indian students.

> Students in grades 8 and 12 were asked to indicate their parents' highest level of education. Consistent with past . . . assessments, students in 1998 who reported higher levels of parental education had higher average reading scale scores.

> The 1998 results by region indicated that fourth and eighth graders in the Northeast and Central regions outperformed their counterparts in the Southeast and West. Among twelfth graders, students in the Southeast had lower average reading scores than students in the other three regions. Also among twelfth graders, students in the Central region outperformed students in the West region.

> In 1998, fourth and eighth graders in central city schools had lower average reading scores than their counterparts in rural/small town schools or urban fringe/large town schools. Also, eighth graders in rural/small town schools had lower average scores than their counterparts in urban fringe/large town schools. No significant differences were observed among twelfth graders by type of location.

> Consistent with past . . . reading assessments, the 1998 results indicated that students attending nonpublic schools had higher average scale scores than their counterparts attending public schools.[19]

Other findings relate to the fact that higher reading scores relate to fewer hours of television watching, teachers giving students books to read, home discussions about student studies, and students talking about reading activities with friends and family.[20]

The 1998 writing report card showed that students were often not writing at their grade level.[21] Students experience problems in expressing themselves through the written word. Extrapolating from these findings, students may not be given sufficient writing opportunities in middle and secondary school as well as when undergraduates.

The conclusion that can be drawn is that students, be they in secondary or higher education, may not have class assignments involving extensive use of library resources. Education may focus more on amassing facts than on engaging in critical thinking and problem solving.

Higher Education

"Higher education is in turbulence," according to Dees Stallings, as it adjusts its "programs and services to meet the needs of both traditional students and the growing population of continuing education students." He states that higher education faces competition from corporate programs and new universities, including the so-called virtual university, which is positioning itself "to meet the needs of a high-tech, diverse, and globally-oriented society."[22] More institutions, as well as companies, are now offering Internet-based courses and programs even for high school students. According to Sarah Carr and Jeffrey R. Young,

> [These] virtual high schools [offer] remedial courses, such as English as a second language, and courses for gifted students, such as advanced composition classes. [The focus is] mainly on advanced placement and college-preparatory courses in the kinds of subjects that many traditional high schools don't have enough teachers or money to offer. Proponents say distance education can give high-school students in poor districts opportunities for advanced classes that have traditionally been available only in upscale areas.[23]

Apparently, a number of these programs and courses offer prepackaged resources for students to use. In a number of instances, adjunct faculty teach these courses, and librarians may be unaware of the nature of class assignments and the resources used. If the faculty expect students to use library resources, where do both faculty and students turn? Does the institution supporting the course or program of study have a library, or does it extend library services to all remote learners?

As more colleges and universities engage in remote teaching and learning through the Internet, they will expect their own libraries to support these offerings, probably without any expansion in budgets. Library budgets will likely remain static or decline. However, librarians will be expected to do more, and faculty and students will have increased expectations, which may make it more difficult for libraries to meet service quality and satisfaction expectations.

Scholarly Communication

Scholarly communication refers to the information exchange occurring among, for instance, faculty and graduate students in higher education. The channels for such communication might be formal publication through scholarly journals and monographs, informal discourse among colleagues, use of digital resources (e.g., the Web and digital libraries), preprint collections, and scholarly conferences and their proceedings. The digitization of information and knowledge is breaking down the traditional means of scholarly communication and disciplinary boundaries as more scholars easily search for and retrieve literature globally from multiple disciplines.

Students and faculty do not need to visit a library in person or remotely; they might be able to find those works or sections of works that they need through services such as those provided by netLibrary (http://www.netlibrary.com). For instance, netLibrary provides access to a wide array of digital books and chapters of books. These works might, but do not necessarily, have a print counterpart.

An example of a forthcoming service likely to have a profound impact on scholarly communication in the physical sciences is a coalition of twelve scientific journal publishers that are interlinking millions of online journal articles. Anyone using the service will be able "to click on a footnote and immediately read the abstract . . . In most cases, the full text of the [cited] article will be available if the researcher's institution has a subscription to the journal or if the journal offers its articles free."[24] Such a service will increase the dependency of researchers in the sciences on the electronic delivery of the journal literature to their office or home computer. Clearly, the education provided by virtual universities and courses taught digitally will increase the demand for libraries to offer more electronically delivered resources. Libraries are already expanding the services that they offer remote users; these users are not limited to students receiving their education digitally. Critical questions become "What roles will libraries play in the future of education? As customer expectations change, how will libraries respond—and how fast will they do so? Will library competitors respond faster and with 'better' services?"

Getting Started with Service Quality and Satisfaction

Chapters 5 and 6 discussed the service plan and how to implement it. At this time, the literature of library and information science does not offer case studies that assess the effectiveness of the plans and pledges of institutions such as Wright State University (see appendix C in chapter 4) and Lehigh University.[25] The purpose of such case studies would be to see what the profession can apply more broadly and the problems in doing so. As shown in this book, there is a viable alternative to SERVQUAL for the measurement of service quality (see figure 2.1), and that alternative is linked to the local planning process. Most definitely, a number of libraries want to improve their customer service.

Libraries wanting to develop a service plan or a pledge should start immediately but modestly. They might hold an all-day staff retreat, or several retreats over time, to review the Wright State University pledge and some of the exercises specified in *The Big Book of Customer Service Training Games*.[26] The purpose of an informal working session would be to explore what everyone is willing to commit to and to identify problems in drafting a pledge and service plan. The intent is to get the staff to talk and interact with each other. Clearly, listening to customers and meeting their expectations ultimately involve a long-term commitment, one in which the library should not overextend its resources. Any library can only do so much, especially with limited resources. Librarians need to

set priorities

manage expectations

work smarter (not necessarily doing things as they have always done)

involve customers in a forward-thinking management process in which they provide the library with regular, meaningful feedback to shape service delivery

Thus, it is important to develop a time chart and move the process from that internal review to the development and implementation of a service plan (see chapter 6).

Accompanying that movement toward implementation of a service plan, management must make a firm commitment to training staff and to challenging the staff to become more customer focused. At some point, the library must invite and encourage customers to be active in the process and to participate in a community view of customer service. First, however, the staff must meet, and the library must see where everyone is and what they are willing to do. Furthermore, the management team must be willing and able to lead.

Educational Rankings

In an interesting article, Ben Gose explains that colleges and universities are seeking their own measures of quality as an alternative to the ranking of institutions by the popular press. These rankings tend to be based on criteria that colleges and universities question; they tend to be subjective without requiring extensive and current knowledge about the specific programs, departments, or institutions being evaluated. As an alternative, the National Survey of Student Engagement will "study undergraduates at 750 colleges over the next three years and use the data to establish national benchmarks for different types of institutions."[27] Russell Edgerton, director of the Education Program at the Pew Charitable Trusts and a proponent of the National Survey, argues that "unless we develop measures of quality where colleges can actually provide evidence of their contributions to student learning, then this whole system [of ranking colleges] turns on resources and reputation, and reinforces the elitism of higher education."[28]

Apparently, examples of questions on the National Survey of Student Engagement include

how many times students were required to make a class presentation

how often they had conversations with professors outside of class

how many times they wrote papers that were at least twenty pages long

whether they would attend the same institution a second time[29]

The last measure is one of satisfaction, but do the other measures truly reflect quality? They focus on whether or not students have, and take advantage of, opportunities for oral and written communication and presume that by engaging in certain activities quality is the outcome. Such simplistic measures are no substitute for outcome assessment (see chapter 4), but they do suggest opportunities for academic libraries to play a role.

Faculty might develop and maintain Web sites for their classes that contain the resources necessary to guide class discussion and complete assignments. Librarians should approach such sites with caution, especially if these sites offer a limited array of resources and if faculty place material subject to copyright restriction on these pages. Quality is more than convenience and must be better linked to learning (and receptivity to learning), including customer expectations.

Achieving Service Quality and Satisfaction

As this chapter suggests, customer expectations are not static—they change over time as customers gain new experiences and are offered new services from a wide assortment of providers. Customers will compare services and select those features they most appreciate. Valarie A. Zeithaml, A. Parasuraman, and Leonard L. Berry identified ten dimensions of service quality:

1. *Tangibles*   appearance of physical facilities, equipment, personnel, and communication materials
2. *Reliability*   ability to perform the promised service dependably and accurately
3. *Responsiveness*   willingness to help customers and to provide prompt service
4. *Courtesy*   politeness, respect, and friendliness of contact personnel
5. *Empathy*   caring and individualized attention that the organization provides its customers
6. *Competence*   required skills and knowledge to perform the service, believability, and honesty of the service provider
7. *Security*   freedom from danger, risk, or doubt
8. *Access*   approachability and ease of contact
9. *Communication*   keeping the customers informed in language they can understand, and listening to them
10. *Understanding the customer*   making the effort to know customers and their needs[30]

As reflected in figure 2.1, tangibles, reliability, responsiveness, assurance, and empathy are dimensions of service quality examined across the service industry. Of these, reliability has tended to be the most important and tangibles the least important. Anyone wanting a link between the instrument depicted in figure 2.1 and SERVQUAL should include all five dimensions. Figure 2.1, therefore, offers a planning tool to assess what is important to meet or exceed the expectations of a library's customers for quality service, a way to monitor how well a library is doing according to its customers, and a tool for comparing general dimensions across service industries.

There is no magical, quick solution demonstrating that customers now and forever are delighted customers who will never experience a service failure. As so many writers indicate, service quality and satisfaction are taken one step and one customer at any time. Still, libraries can plan and anticipate expectations, settling on those they can meet well and explaining why they cannot meet others with the same high quality. Within this context, it might be better to suggest that libraries can achieve a level of service quality and satisfaction but that retaining the same level over time (not necessarily exceeding the level) will require daily attention. Perhaps, then, libraries might best be advised to make an ongoing commitment to achieving service quality and satisfaction.

Summary

Librarians need to listen to customers and to be guided by their organization's vision and mission statements as well as goals and objectives. Vision and mission statements are no longer a luxury; they are essential for libraries trying to delight customers, and, in some instances, stakeholders, with those services provided in fiscally stringent times. The library without walls only expands the potential number of expectations that it might be called upon to meet. Clearly, expectations are like a moving target; they shift over time. Libraries need strategies and tools for coping with changing expectations and finding those instances where they can delight customers. Planning and accountability are two essential aspects that underpin the embracing of service quality and satisfaction. Creating a service plan does not require the resources necessary to undertake a comprehensive strategic plan (although any strategic plan should include a service plan component).

Libraries that use the strategies and tools presented in this book will be better able to manage the satisfaction relationship, delight their customers, and evolve a mission that indeed ensures that the library assumes a prized place in the community.

A measure of library quality based solely on collections has become obsolete.[31]

NOTES

1. *StatPac for Windows* (Minneapolis, Minn.: StatPac, 1999), 7.
2. Amy K. Smith, Ruth N. Bolton, and Janet Wagner, "A Model of Customer Satisfaction with Service Encounters Involving Failure and Recovery," *Journal*

of Marketing Research 36, no. 7 (August 1999): 356. Available: http://web5. infotrac.galegroup.com/...yn=14!xm_19_0_A55698106?sw_aep=ntn.

3. Karen Hyman, "Customer Service and the 'Rule of 1965,'" *American Libraries* 30, no. 9 (Oct. 1999): 58.

4. Ibid.

5. Patricia A. Knowles, Stephen J. Grove, and Gregory M. Pickett, "Mood versus Service Quality Effects on Customers' Responses to Service Organizations and Service Encounters," *Journal of Service Research* 2, no. 2 (Nov. 1999): 187, 197.

6. Ibid., 197.

7. Ibid.

8. Andrew Odlyzko, "Competition and Cooperation: Libraries and Publishers in the Transition to Electronic Scholarly Journals," *Journal of Scholarly Publishing* 30, no. 4 (July 1999): 163.

9. Ibid., 181.

10. Will Weissert, "Public Believes in America's Colleges but Not in Its Schools, a Study Concludes," in *Today's News [The Chronicle of Higher Education]* (21 Oct. 1999): 1. Available: http://chronicle.com/daily/99/10/99102106n.htm.

11. U.S. Bureau of the Census, "Resident Population Estimates of the United States by Age and Sex: April 1, 1990 to August 1, 1999." Available: http://www.census.gov/population/estimates/nation/intfile2-1.txt (release date: 1 Oct. 1999).

12. See U.S. Bureau of the Census, "Resident Population of the United States: Middle Series Projections, 2001–2005, by Age and Sex." Available: http://www.census.gov/population/projections/nation/nas/npas0105.txt (release date: March 1999); U.S. Bureau of the Census, "Resident Population of the United States: Middle Series Projections, 2001–2005, by Sex, Race, and Hispanic Origin, with Median Age." Available: http://www.census.gov/population/projections/nation/nsrh/nprh0105.txt (release date: March 1996).

13. "Increase in At-Home Workers Reverses Earlier Trend," *Census Brief* (Washington, D.C.: Bureau of the Census, March 1998), 1, 2.

14. U.S. Bureau of the Census, "Educational Attainment in the United States: March 1998 (Update)," *Current Population Reports*, P20-513 (Washington, D.C.: The Bureau, Oct. 1998).

15. U.S. Department of Education, National Center for Education Statistics, "Dropout Rates Remain Stable over Last Decade" (press release, 17 Dec. 1997). Available: http://nces.ed.gov/Pressrelease/dropout.html.

16. National Institute for Literacy, "Fast Facts on Literacy" (Washington, D.C.: National Institute for Literacy, 1999). Available: http://nifl.gov/newwprld/FASFACT.HTM.

17. See Cheryl Metoyer-Duran, *Gatekeepers in Ethnolinguistic Communities* (Norwood, N.J.: Ablex, 1993); Cheryl Metoyer-Duran, "Cross-Cultural Research in Ethnolinguistic Communities: Methodological Considerations," *Public Libraries* 32, no. 1 (Jan./Feb. 1993): 18–25.

18. U.S. Department of Education, National Center for Education Statistics, "The Nation's Report Card: NAEP 1998 Reading Report Card for the Nation and the States" (March 1999), 2. Available: http://nces.ed.gov/nationsreportcard/pubs/main1998/1999500.shtml.

19. Ibid., 2–3.

20. Ibid., 4–5.

21. U.S. Department of Education, National Center for Education Statistics, "NAEP 1998 Writing: Report Card for the Nation and the States" (Sept. 1999). Available: http://nces.ed.gov/pubsearch/pubsinfo.asp?pubid=1999462.

22. Dees Stallings, "The Virtual University Is Inevitable: But Will the Model Be Non-Profit or Profit? A Speculative Commentary on the Emerging Education Environment," *Journal of Academic Librarianship* 23, no. 4 (July 1997): 271.

23. Sarah Carr and Jeffrey R. Young, "As Distance-Learning Boom Spreads, Colleges Help Set up Virtual High Schools," *The Chronicle of Higher Education* XLVI, no. 9 (22 Oct. 1999): A55.

24. See Kelly McCollum, "Publishers of On-Line Journals Plan to Link Millions of Science Footnotes," *The Chronicle of Higher Education* XLVI, no. 14 (26 Nov. 1999): A68. The coalition now includes John Wiley and Sons, Academic Press, the American Association for the Advancement of Science, the American Institute of Physics, the Association for Computing Machinery, Blackwell Science, Elsevier Science, the Institute of Electrical and Electronics Engineers, Kluwer Academic Publishers, Nature, Oxford University Press, and Springer-Verlag.

25. "Lehigh University Information Resources Service Standards," in Peter Hernon and Ellen Altman, *Assessing Service Quality: Satisfying the Expectations of Library Customers* (Chicago: American Library Assn., 1998), 39–41.

26. Peggy Carlaw and Vasudha Kathleen Deming, *The Big Book of Customer Service Training Games* (New York: McGraw-Hill, 1999).

27. Ben Gose, "A New Survey of 'Good Practices' Could Be an Alternative to Rankings," *The Chronicle of Higher Education* XLVI, no. 9 (22 Oct. 1999): A65.

28. Ibid.

29. Ibid.

30. Adapted with the permission of The Free Press, a Division of Simon & Schuster, from *Delivering Quality Service: Balancing Customer Perceptions and Expectations* by Valarie A. Zeithaml, A. Parasuraman, and Leonard L. Berry, 22–3, 26. Copyright © 1999 by Leonard L. Berry.

31. Danuta A. Nitecki, "Changing the Concept and Measure of Service Quality in Academic Libraries," *Journal of Academic Librarianship* 22, no. 3 (May 1996): 181.

Bibliography

Abend, Jennifer, and Charles R. McClure. "Recent Views on Identifying Impacts from Public Libraries." *Public Library Quarterly* 17, no. 3 (1999): 3–29.

Achieving Breakthrough Service in Libraries. A Nationwide Teleseminar Presented by the American Library Association. Cambridge, Mass.: Kathleen Gilroy Assoc., 1994.

"ACRL Guidelines for Extended Campus Library Services." *College & Research Libraries News* 51, no. 4 (April 1990): 353–5.

Aitkins, Jo. "Setting Standards and Monitoring Performance: The Experience of Information Series at the University of Sunderland." In *Proceedings of the 2nd Northumbria International Conference on Performance Measurement in Libraries and Information Services,* 101–4. Newcastle upon Tyne, Eng.: Information North, 1998.

Aleamoni, L. M. "Student Ratings of Instruction." In *Handbook of Teacher Evaluation,* edited by J. Millman, 110–145. Beverly Hills, Calif.: Sage, 1981.

Altman, Ellen, and Peter Hernon, eds. *Research Misconduct: Issues, Implications, and Strategies.* Greenwich, Conn.: Ablex, 1997.

———. "Service Quality and Customer Satisfaction Do Matter." *American Libraries* 29, no. 7 (Aug. 1998): 53–4.

American Library Assn., Committee on Accreditation. *Outcomes Assessment for Library and Information Studies: Resource Manual.* Chicago: American Library Assn., 1995.

Ary, Donald, Lucy C. Jacobs, and Asghar Razavieh. *Introduction to Research in Education.* 3d ed. New York: Rinehart and Winston, 1985.

Assn. of College and Research Libraries. "Information Literacy Competency Standards for Higher Education." Chicago: American Library Assn., n.d. Available: http://www.ala.org/acrl/ilstandardlo.html.

———. Task Force on Academic Library Outcomes Assessment. *Report* (June 27, 1998). Available: http://www.ala.org/acrl/outcome.html.

Berry, Leonard L. *Discovering the Soul of Service: The New Drivers of Sustainable Business Success.* New York: The Free Press, 1999.

Bitner, Mary Jo, and Amy R. Hubert. "Encounter Satisfaction versus Overall Satisfaction versus Quality." In *Service Quality: New Directions in Theory and Practice,* edited by Roland T. Rust and Richard L. Oliver, 72–94. Thousand Oaks, Calif.: Sage, 1994.

Blalock, Hubert M., Jr. *Social Statistics.* New York: McGraw-Hill, 1972.

Bottrill, Karen V., and Victor M. H. Borden. "Appendix: Examples from the Literature." *New Directions for Institutional Research* 82 (summer 1994): 107–17.

Busha, Charles H., and Stephen P. Harter. *Research Methods for Librarianship: Techniques and Interpretation.* New York: Academic Press, 1980.

Carlaw, Peggy, and Vasudha Kathleen Deming. *The Big Book of Customer Service Training Games*. New York: McGraw-Hill, 1999.

Carlzon, Jan. *Moments of Truth*. New York: Harper-Collins, 1987.

Carr, Sarah, and Jeffrey R. Young. "As Distance-Learning Boom Spreads, Colleges Help Set up Virtual High Schools." *The Chronicle of Higher Education* XLVI, no. 9 (22 Oct. 1999): A55–A57.

Chen, Ching-chih, and Peter Hernon. *Information Seeking: Assessing and Anticipating User Needs*. New York: Neal-Schuman, 1982.

Childers, Thomas A., and Nancy A. Van House. *What's Good? Describing Your Public Library's Effectiveness*. Chicago: American Library Assn., 1993.

Chisholm, John. "Using the Internet to Measure Customer Satisfaction and Loyalty." In *Best Practices in Customer Service*, edited by Ron Zemke and John A. Woods, 305–17. New York: American Management Assn., 1999.

Cox, Allan B., and Fred Gifford. "An Overview to Geographic Information Systems." *Journal of Academic Librarianship* 23, no. 6 (Nov. 1997): 449–61.

Davidow, William H., and Bro Uttal. *Total Customer Service: The Ultimate Weapon*. New York: Harper Perennial, 1989.

Dickeson, Robert C. *Prioritizing Academic Programs and Services: Reallocating Resources to Achieve Strategic Balance*. San Francisco: Jossey-Bass, 1999.

Dillman, Don A., Robert D. Tortora, and Dennis Bowker. "Principles for Constructing Web Surveys" (1999). Available (WebSurveyor™): http://www.websurveyor.com/home_tios.asp.

Duffy, Jo Ann M., and Alice A. Ketchand. "Examining the Role of Service Quality in Overall Service Satisfaction." *Journal of Managerial Issues* 10, no. 2 (summer 1998): 240–8.

EQUINOX. "Initial Definition of Electronic Performance Indicators." Available: http://equinox.dcu.ie/reports/pilist.html.

Franklin, Hardy R. "Customer Service: The Heart of a Library." In *Libraries Change Lives: 1994 Campaign Book Supplement*, 8. Chicago: American Library Assn., 1993.

Freed, Jann E., and Marie R. Klugman. *Quality Principles and Practices in Higher Education: Different Questions for Different Times*. Phoenix, Ariz.: Oryx, 1997.

Fromm, Bill, and Len Schlesinger. *The Real Heroes of Business: And Not a CEO among Them*. New York: Doubleday, 1993.

Gose, Ben. "A New Survey of 'Good Practices' Could Be an Alternative to Rankings." *The Chronicle of Higher Education* XLVI, no. 9 (22 Oct. 1999): A65–A67.

Granger, Charles H. "The Hierarchy of Objectives." *Harvard Business Review* 42, no. 3 (May–June 1964): 63–74.

Grimes, Deborah J. *Academic Library Centrality: User Success through Service, Access, and Tradition*. Chicago: American Library Assn., Assn. of College and Research Libraries, 1998.

"Guidelines for University Undergraduate Libraries." *College & Research Libraries News* 58, no. 5 (May 1997): 330–3.

Hafner, Arthur W. *Descriptive Statistical Techniques for Librarians*. 2d ed. Chicago: American Library Assn., 1998.

Hastreiter, Jamie A., Marsha Cornelius, and David W. Henderson. *Mission Statements for College Libraries*. 2d ed. Chicago: American Library Assn., Assn. of College and Research Libraries, 1999.

Hawkins, Brian L. "Distributed Learning and Institutional Restructuring." *Educom Review* 34, no. 4 (July/Aug. 1999): 12–15, 42–4.

Hernon, Peter. *Statistics: A Component of the Research Process*. Norwood, N.J.: Ablex, 1994.

Hernon, Peter, and Ellen Altman. *Assessing Service Quality: Satisfying the Expectations of Library Customers*. Chicago: American Library Assn., 1998.

———. *Service Quality in Academic Libraries*. Norwood, N.J.: Ablex, 1996.

Hernon, Peter, and Charles R. McClure. *Evaluation and Library Decision Making*. Norwood, N.J.: Ablex, 1990.

Hernon, Peter, Danuta Nitecki, and Ellen Altman. "Service Quality and Customer Satisfaction: An Assessment and Future Directions." *Journal of Academic Librarianship* 25, no. 1 (Jan. 1999): 9–17.

Heskett, James L., W. Earl Sasser Jr., and Leonard A. Schlesinger. *The Service Profit Chain: How Leading Companies Link Profit and Growth to Loyalty, Satisfaction, and Value*. New York: The Free Press, 1997.

Himmel, Ethel, and William James Wilson, with the ReVision Committee of the Public Library Association. *Planning for Results: A Public Library Transformation Process: The Guidebook*. Chicago: American Library Assn., 1998.

———. *Planning for Results: A Public Library Transformation Process: How-to-Do-It Manual.* Chicago: American Library Assn., 1998.

Hirshon, Arnold. "Libraries, Consortia, and Change Management." *Journal of Academic Librarianship* 25, no. 2 (March 1999): 124–6.

Hoadley, Irene B. "Reflections: Management Morphology—How We Get to Be Who We Are." *Journal of Academic Librarianship* 25, no, 4 (July 1999): 267–73.

Holbrook, Morris B. "The Nature of Customer Value: An Axiology of Services in the Consumption Experience." In *Service Quality: New Directions in Theory and Practice*, edited by Roland T. Rust and Richard L. Oliver, 21–71. Thousand Oaks, Calif.: Sage, 1994.

Holt, Glen E., Donald Elliott, and Amonia Moore. "Placing a Value on Public Library Services." *Public Libraries* 38, no. 2 (March/April 1999): 98–108.

Hyman, Karen. "Customer Service and the 'Rule of 1965.'" *American Libraries* 30, no. 9 (Oct. 1999): 54, 56–8.

"Increase in At-Home Workers Reverses Earlier Trend." *Census Brief.* Washington, D.C.: Bureau of the Census, March 1998.

"Indiana University Bloomington Libraries Mission and Vision." Bloomington: Indiana University, 1997. Available: http://www.indiana.edu/~libadmin/mission.html.

Information and Documentation—Library Performance Indicators. Geneva, Switz.: International Organization for Standardization, 1998.

Isaac, Stephen, and William B. Michael. *Handbook in Research and Evaluation.* 3d ed. San Diego, Calif.: EdiTS, 1995.

Johnson, Michael D. *Customer Orientation and Market Action.* Upper Saddle River, N.J.: Prentice-Hall, 1998.

Knowles, Patricia A., Stephen J. Grove, and Gregory M. Pickett. "Mood versus Service Quality Effects on Customers' Responses to Service Organizations and Service Encounters." *Journal of Service Research* 2, no. 2 (Nov. 1999): 187–99.

Lakos, Amos. "Building a Culture of Assessment in Academic Libraries—Obstacles and Possibilities." Paper presented at Living the Future II, Tucson, Ariz., 22 April 1998.

"Lehigh University Information Resources Service Standards." In Peter Hernon and Ellen Altman, *Assessing Service Quality: Satisfying the Expectations of Library Customers*, 39–41. Chicago: American Library Assn., 1998.

Leisner, Tony. "Mission Statements and the Marketing Mix." *Public Libraries* 25, no, 3 (fall 1986): 86–7.

Lindauer, Bonnie Gratch. "Defining and Measuring the Library's Impact on Campuswide Outcomes." *College & Research Libraries* 59, no. 6 (Nov. 1998): 546–70.

McCollum, Kelly. "Publishers of On-Line Journals Plan to Link Millions of Science Footnotes." *The Chronicle of Higher Education* XLVI, no. 14 (26 Nov. 1999): A68.

McClure, Charles R. "So What Are the Impacts of Networking on Academic Institutions." *Internet Research* 4, no. 2 (summer 1994): 2–6.

Marsh, H. W. "Students' Evaluations of University Teaching: Dimensionality, Reliability, Validity, Potential Biases and Utility." *Journal of Educational Psychology* 76 (1984): 707–54.

———. "Students' Evaluations of University Teaching: Research Findings, Methodological Issues, and Directions for Future Research." *International Journal of Educational Research* 11 (1987): 253–88.

Metoyer-Duran, Cheryl. "Cross-Cultural Research in Ethnolinguistic Communities: Methodological Considerations." *Public Libraries* 32, no. 1 (Jan./Feb. 1993): 18–25.

———. *Gatekeepers in Ethnolinguistic Communities.* Norwood, N.J.: Ablex, 1993.

Miller, Rush, and Peter X. Zhou. "Global Resource Sharing: A Gateway Model." *Journal of Academic Librarianship* 25, no. 4 (July 1999): 281–7.

"The Mission of a University Undergraduate Library: Model Statement." *College & Research Libraries News* 48, no. 9 (Oct. 1987): 542–4.

Montanelli, Dale S., and Patricia F. Stenstrom, eds. *People Come First: User-Centered Academic Library Services.* Chicago: American Library Assn., Assn. of College and Research Libraries, 1999.

Mosley, Madison M., Jr. "Mission Statements for the Community College LRC." *College & Research Libraries News* 49, no. 10 (Nov. 1988): 653–4.

National Institute for Literacy. "Fast Facts on Literacy." Washington, D.C.: National Institute for Literacy, 1999. Available: http://www.nifl.gov/newworld/FASTFACT.HTM.

Nelson, Sandra, Ellen Altman, and Diane Mayo. *Managing for Results: Effective Resource Allocation for Public Libraries.* Chicago: American Library Assn., 2000.

Nitecki, Danuta A. "Changing the Concept and Measure of Service Quality in Academic Libraries." *Journal of Academic Librarianship* 22, no. 3 (May 1996): 181–90.

Nitecki, Danuta, and Peter Hernon. "Measuring Service Quality at Yale University's Library." *Journal of Academic Librarianship* 26 (July 2000): 259–73.

Odlyzko, Andrew. "Competition and Cooperation: Libraries and Publishers in the Transition to Electronic Scholarly Journals." *Journal of Scholarly Publishing* 30, no. 4 (July 1999): 163–85.

Palomba, Catherine A., and Trudy W. Banta. *Assessment Essentials: Planning, Implementing Assessment in Higher Education.* San Francisco: Jossey-Bass, 1999.

Pillemer, David B. *Momentous Events, Vivid Memories: How Unforgettable Moments Help Us Understand the Meaning of Our Lives.* Cambridge, Mass.: Harvard University Press, 1998.

Powell, Ronald R. *Basic Research Methods for Librarians.* 3d ed. Greenwich, Conn.: Ablex, 1997.

Rosenblatt, Susan. "Information Technology Investments in Research Libraries." *Educom Review* 34, no. 4 (July/Aug. 1999): 28-32, 44-6.

Rossi, Peter H., Howard E. Freeman, and Mark W. Lipsey. *Evaluation: A Systematic Approach.* 6th ed. Thousand Oaks, Calif.: Sage, 1999.

Smith, Amy K., Ruth N. Bolton, and Janet Wagner. "A Model of Customer Service Satisfaction with Service Encounters Involving Failure and Recovery." *Journal of Marketing Research* 36, no. 7 (Aug. 1999): 356. Available: http://web5.infotrac.galegroup.com/...yn=14!xm_19_0_A55698106?sw_aep=ntn.

Smith, Susan. "How to Create a Plan to Deliver Great Service." In *Best Practices in Customer Service,* edited by Ron Zemke and John A. Woods, 55–66. New York: AMACOM, 1999.

St. Joseph's County Public Library. "SJCPL's List of Public Libraries with WWW Services." Available: http://sjcpl.lib.in.us/homepage/PublicLibraries/PublicLibraryServers.html.

Stafford, Marla Royne. "A Normative Model for Improving Services Quality." *Journal of Customer Services in Marketing & Management* 1, no. 1 (1994): 13–30.

Stallings, Dees. "The Virtual University Is Inevitable: But Will the Model Be Non-Profit or Profit? A Speculative Commentary on the Emerging Education Environment," *Journal of Academic Librarianship* 23, no. 4 (July 1997): 271–80.

"Standards for College Libraries: A Draft." *College & Research Libraries News* 60, no. 5 (May 1999): 377–81.

"Standards for Community, Junior, and Technical College Learning Resources Program." *College & Research Libraries News* 55, no. 9 (Sept. 1994): 572–85.

"Standards for University Libraries: Evaluation of Performance." *College & Research Libraries News* 50, no. 8 (Aug. 1989): 679–91.

Stauss, Bernd, and Christian Friege. "Regaining Service Customers." *Journal of Service Research* 1, no. 4 (May 1999): 347–61.

Stueart, Robert D., and Barbara B. Moran. *Library and Information Center Management.* 5th ed. Englewood, Colo.: Libraries Unlimited, 1998.

Suffolk University, Sawyer Library. "Strategic Plan, July 1, 1999–June 30, 2002." Boston, Mass.: Suffolk University, 1999.

Swisher, Robert, and Charles R. McClure. *Research for Decision Making: Methods for Librarians.* Chicago: American Library Assn., 1984.

Tufte, Edward R. *The Visual Display of Quantitative Information.* Cheshire, Vt.: Graphics Press, 1983.

University of Maryland Libraries. "Libraries' Mission." College Park, Md.: The University. Available: http://www.lib.umd.edu/UMCP/PUB/mission.html.

University of Michigan Business School, National Quality Research Center. *The American Customer Satisfaction Index: Methodology Report.* Milwaukee: American Society for Quality, 1998.

University of North Carolina at Chapel Hill, Health Sciences Library. "Strategic Plan." Chapel Hill, N.C.: University of North Carolina at Chapel Hill, 1990.

University of Phoenix, Department of Institutional Research. "Assessment Systems for Measuring Student Achievement and Improving Institutional Effectiveness." Phoenix, Ariz.: University of Phoenix, n.d. Brochure.

"The University of Pittsburgh." *Academe Today's Daily Report [The Chronicle of Higher Education]* (29 Jan. 1999). Available: http://chronicle.com.

U.S. Bureau of the Census. "Educational Attainment in the United States: March 1998 (Update)." *Current Population Reports,* P20-513. Washington, D.C.: The Bureau, Oct. 1998.

———. "Resident Population Estimates of the United States by Age and Sex: April 1, 1990 to August 1,

1999." Washington, D.C.: The Bureau, 1 Oct. 1999. Available: http://www.census.gov/population/estimates/nation/intfile2-1.txt.

———. "Resident Population of the United States: Middle Series Projections, 2001–2005, by Age and Sex." Washington D.C.: The Bureau, March 1996. Available: http://www.census.gov/population/projections/nation/nas/npas0105.txt. (Mar. 1999.)

———. "Resident Population of the United States: Middle Series Projections, 2001–2005, by Sex, Race, and Hispanic Origin, with Median Age." Washington, D.C.: The Bureau, (March 1999). Available: http://www.census.gov/population/projections/nation/nsrh/nprh0105.txt.

U.S. Department of Education, National Center for Education Statistics. "Dropout Rates Remain Stable over Last Decade." Press release. Washington, D.C.: The Department, 17 Dec. 1997. Available: http://nces.ed.gov/Pressrelease/dropout.html.

———. "NAEP 1998 Writing: Report Card for the Nation and the States." Washington, D.C.: The Department, Sept. 1999. Available: http://nces.ed.gov/pubsearch/pubsinfo.asp?pubid=1999462.

———. "The Nation's Report Card: NAEP 1998 Reading Report Card for the Nation and the States." Washington, D.C.: The Department, March 1999. Available: http://nces.ed.gov/nationsreportcard/pubs/main1998/1999500.shtml.

U.S. General Accounting Office, Program Evaluation and Methodology Div. *Quantitative Data Analysis: An Introduction.* Washington, D.C.: The Office, 1992.

U.S. National Performance Review. *Putting Customers First: Standards for Serving the American People.* Washington, D.C.: GPO, 1994.

———. *Serving the American Public: Best Practices in Customer-Driven Strategic Planning.* Washington, D.C.: National Performance Review, 1997.

———. *World-Class Courtesy: A Best Practices Report.* Washington, D.C.: GPO, 1997. Available: http://www.npr.gov/library/papers/benchmrk/courtesy/chapter1.html.

U.S. Office of Management and Budget, "Primer on Performance Measurement." Washington, D.C.: The Office, 28 Feb. 1995. Available: ftp://ftp.fedworld.gov/pub/results/primer01.txt.

Walters, Suzanne. *Customer Service: A How-to-Do-It Manual for Librarians.* New York: Neal-Schuman, 1994.

Wehmeyer, Susan, Dorothy Auchter, and Arnold Hirshon. "Saying What We Will Do, and Doing What We Say: Implementing a Customer Service Plan." *Journal of Academic Librarianship* 22, no. 3 (May 1996): 173–80.

Weingand, Darlene E. *Customer Service Excellence: A Concise Guide for Librarians.* Chicago: American Library Assn., 1997.

Weiss, Carol H., and Michael J. Bucuvalas. "Truth Tests and Utility Tests: Decision-Makers' Frames of Reference for Social Science Research." *American Sociological Review* 45, no. 2 (April 1980): 302–13.

Weissert, Will. "Public Believes in America's Colleges but Not in Its Schools, a Study Concludes." In *Today's News [The Chronicle of Higher Education]* (21 Oct. 1999). Available: http://chronicle.com/daily/99/10/99102106n.htm.

Whitman, John R. *The Beneserve Customer Satisfaction System.* Wellesley, Mass.: Surveytools Corp., 1998.

———. *The Benevox Public Satisfaction System.* Wellesley, Mass.: Surveytools Corp., 1998.

———. *Customer Focus at the Los Alamos National Laboratory Research Library: "Understand 'em and Give It to 'em!"* Wellesley, Mass.: Surveytools Corp., 1999.

———. *How to Be an Outstanding Service Employee.* Wellesley, Mass.: Surveytools Corp., 1999.

Wiehl, Peggy. *William D. Ruckelshaus and the Environmental Protection Agency.* Case #9-375-083. Rev. 5/78. Boston, Mass.: Harvard University Intercollegiate Case Clearing House, 1974.

Wright State University Libraries. "Commitment to Excellence." Dayton, Ohio: Wright State University Libraries, 1999. Available: http://www.libraries.wright.edu/services/Customer_Services.html.

———. "Diversity Vision Statement." Dayton, Ohio: Wright State University Libraries, 1999. Available: http://www.libraries.wright.edu/policies/diversity.html.

"Wright State University Libraries' Pledge and Commitment to Excellence." In Peter Hernon and Ellen Altman, *Service Quality in Academic Libraries,* 59–60. Norwood, N.J.: Ablex, 1996.

Zemke, Ron, and John A. Woods, eds. *Best Practices in Customer Service.* New York: AMACOM, 1999.

Zeithaml, Valarie A., A. Parasuraman, and Leonard L. Berry. *Delivering Quality Service: Balancing Customer Perceptions and Expectations.* New York: The Free Press, 1999.

Index

Note: Page references to figures and tables are in *italics*.

Peter Hernon is professor, Graduate School of Library and Information Science, Simmons College, Boston, where he teaches courses related to research methods, evaluation of library services, and government information. Hernon received his Ph.D. from Indiana University, Bloomington, in 1978. He is the editor-in-chief of the *Journal of Academic Librarianship*, founding editor of *Government Information Quarterly*, and coeditor of *Library & Information Science Research*. Hernon is the author or editor of 35 books and more than 120 articles. His coauthored book *Assessing Service Quality* was the 1999 recipient of the Highsmith Library Literature Award.

John R. Whitman is founder and president of Surveytools Corporation, a survey research firm in Wellesley, Massachusetts, and founder of several software and Internet publishing ventures. He conducts seminars and workshops on several topics, including creating and measuring customer satisfaction. Whitman has carried out numerous satisfaction and customer research studies for private and public sector firms and institutions, including libraries of various types and sizes, and has developed several software products. He is the author of the *Beneserve Customer Satisfaction System* for businesses of all sizes and the *Benevox Public Satisfaction System* for public educational facilities, both published by Surveytools. He holds a Master of Education degree from Harvard University.